Glasgow
by the way, but

Celebrating a City

Glasgow
by the way, but

Celebrating a City

JOHN CAIRNEY

Luath Press Limited
EDINBURGH
www.luath.co.uk

First published 2006

The paper used in this book is recyclable. It is made from low chlorine
pulps produced in a low energy, low emission manner from
renewable forests.

Typeset in Sabon 10.5

ISBN (10): 1-905222-50-5
ISBN (13): 978-1-9-0522250-6

Printed and bound in Great Britain by
Biddles Ltd., King's Lynn, Norfolk

To my brother,
Jim,
who knows what I mean.

Contents

Acknowledgements

THE AUTHOR IS INDEBTED to the Right Honourable Lord Provost of Glasgow and Lord Lieutenant, Liz Cameron, MA for the favour of her foreword and to the good efforts on my behalf of Jim Mearns, one of her staff. I am also grateful to Bill Campbell and Peter MacKenzie of Mainstream Publishing (Edinburgh) for permission to use material from my biography *East End to West End*, and to Alastair Bruce for the use of extracts from my articles for The Tartan Umbrella.

Extensive reference was made to *The Glasgow Encyclopedia*, compiled by Joe Fisher, from the archives of the Mitchell Library and to Michael Munro's *The Patter*, published by Glasgow Libraries and Canongate Publishing, Edinburgh, for specific facts and general information.

Immediate acknowledgement must be made of the first-rate work done by my editor, Catriona Vernal, of Luath Press.

I also wish to express my thanks to the many fellow-Glaswegians, neo-Glaswegians and non-Glaswegians who gave me the benefit of their opinions, anecdotes and downright lies about my home town. They are:

Bob Adams, Louise Annand, Strachan Birnie, Nell Brennan, Jim Cairney, Gordon Cockburn, John and Rosie Coleman, Michael Donnelly, the late Ian Fleming, Ian and Pat Laing, Gordon Irving, Starley Lee, Tony Matteo, Dr Ronald Mavor, Brian McGeachan, Jeanette McGinn, Dr Gerald McGrath, David McKail, John Moore, the late Anthony F. Murray, James Murray, Dr Mike Paterson and Philip Raskin.

Thanks are also due to Appleseed Music, New York for permission to reproduce lyrics by Matt McGinn, and to Scottish Screen for information on the Greens, to Will Fyffe (Junior) for details of his father and I Belong to Glasgow, to Dr James A. Mackay for his help with the Robert W. Service poem quoted and to Sean Cairney of *The Scottish Banner* in Australia for helpful sources. All other verse in the text, apart from traditional material, is my own.

Finally, I must acknowledge the New Zealand contribution, particularly the assistance given by David and Karen Curtis, Max Cryer,

Katie Scott, Colleen Trolove, Katrina Hobbs and, most of all, the life support given me by my wife and first reader, Alannah O'Sullivan. I thank her for her pertinent suggestions at a vital stage in the project and trust that the finished volume you now hold in your hand repays all her efforts on my behalf.

I only hope that it is worth the experience, learning, talent, encouragement and co-operation given to me by everyone named above. If it isn't, the fault is entirely mine.

John Cairney
Auckland, New Zealand, September 2006

Foreword

AT THE RISK OF embarrassing the author, I think it is fair to say that John Cairney is a bit of a Glasgow institution. His skills as an actor and an orator have enthralled many an audience and, like his native city, he has the great ability to re-invent himself. He has crafted careers in the theatre, in television and cinema and is now a successful author. Having made a world-renowned contribution to promoting the works of Scotland's greatest poet, Robert Burns, he has in recent years turned his talents to promoting the works of Scotland's greatest architect, Charles Rennie Mackintosh. John Cairney is indeed a man of many faces, but he is fundamentally a Glaswegian, and Glaswegians love Glasgow.

Glasgow is a city of contrasts where a great deal has been achieved and a great deal remains to be done but, as author Cairney shows, it is also a place where dreams are realised. This book tells many tales of the city on the Clyde and it carries the voice of one of Glasgow's greatest sons. It is a tale of love and adventure, of struggle and progress and of insights and visions.

This year the people of Glasgow have been marvelling at the lovingly restored Kelvingrove Art Gallery and Museum. They have also celebrated the re-opening of their City Halls as a concert venue and many have visited the refurbished Kibble Palace at the Botanic Gardens. Their rebirth for new generations is a significant symbol of the city's ongoing desire to re-invent itself to meet the challenges of the times. Glasgow is, of course, more than simply a collection of great buildings.

John Cairney understands – and demonstrates here – that Glasgow is a city of many voices. It is the welcoming city; a city of architecture, a city of parks, a city of sports but it is above all the dear green place enjoyed by its citizens. It can also be an angry city and it bears the scars of many battles – economic, social and physical – but Glasgow fights on and fights with all the wit and humour at her disposal.

Like John, I am a Glaswegian born and bred. We belong to Glasgow and, even without a drink on a Saturday, we know that Glasgow belongs to us and it's a love story that lasts a lifetime. I have the greatest pleasure in inviting you to read this tale of John Cairney's romance with Glasgow. It's pure dead brilliant, *by the way, but*!

Liz Cameron, Lord Provost of Glasgow

Preamble

IN AUGUST 2004 I was in Edinburgh, appearing at that venerable city's International Book Festival in Charlotte Square with my biography, *The Quest for Robert Louis Stevenson*. I shared a platform with Argentinian writer Alberto Manguel, who had also written about Stevenson in *Under the Palm Trees*, a novel based on Stevenson's time in Samoa. At that time, my RLS book had inched its way, fleetingly, into the Scottish Bestsellers list, and my publisher, Gavin MacDougall of Luath Press in Edinburgh, decided to celebrate with lunch at the Doric Tavern in Market Street with, as he said, RLS paying.

We were joined that day by a mutual friend, secretary of the Edinburgh RLS Club, Dr Alan Marchbank. Talking about Stevenson as we did all through the first course, Alan happened to mention that, while in London and Paris between June and December 1878, Stevenson had written a series of articles for the *Portfolio* magazine which were published in book form as *Edinburgh: Picturesque Notes*. Stevenson, apparently, had been amused to find that not only had the volume managed to offend many of his fellow citizens, it also delighted the same number of Glaswegians, if only for the fact that the essays had annoyed their rivals in Edinburgh. Stevenson's later comment regarding his compatriots, who had to live daily among the Old Town's tall precipices and the New Town's terraced gardens, was succinct:

> Let them console themselves – they do as well as anyone else; the population of (let us say) Chicago would cut quite as rueful a figure on the same romantic stage. To the Glasgow people I would say only one word, but that is of gold: *I have not yet written a book about Glasgow.*

Well, at Alan's suggestion, and with Gavin's approval, I have, and here it is; part polemic, part history, part anecdote, part commentary, part fancy, part autobiography – but what the whole thing amounts to is a Glasgow quilt of many colours. Perhaps these very personal flourishes of mine might be more picaresque than picturesque, but that's Glasgow.

Introduction

Every place is a centre to the earth, whence highways radiate or ships set sail for foreign ports; the limit of the parish is not more imaginary than the frontier of an empire; and, as a man sitting at home in his cabinet and swiftly writing books, so a city sends abroad an influence and a portrait of herself.
ROBERT LOUIS STEVENSON

THIS IS MY SAY. It is a very personal say at that. This is *my* Glasgow – Glasgow as I see it now, now and then, and as I see it in my mind's eye from the other side of the world. These verbal flourishes are by no means intended as a clean sweep; each is the touch of a brush on various aspects of my native city as they occur to me. Mine is only one man's point of view, of course, but it's the kind of happy journey that takes me down the broad avenues of verifiable fact while also giving me the chance to nip down the many side streets of anecdote. It's from this memory-bank that people and places pop up to give flesh and blood to the bare bones of recollection. They also add some colour to the grey shades of objectivity.

Not that I can be anything other than subjective about the place where I grew up. I may now live thousands of miles beyond Glasgow, but the city has been a part of me for too long to allow me to distance myself completely. I still travel the world a good deal but, wherever I go, Glasgow is still at my centre. It is in every part of me, and has been all my life. Both of us may have changed a bit in that time, but I know the essential Glasgow boy is still in me yet, because I can hear his voice. He nags at my subconscious, reminding me of who I really am. He affects everything I say and do, even the way I think about things. It is this inner persona that gives me the continuing sense of where I come from no matter where I've been. It is an awareness I can never be rid of, so I've had to learn to live with it. The good thing is I can call on it wherever I am, and it appears like a genie from a bottle – the only difference being that I do its will, it doesn't do mine.

So I have come to recognise that it will be part of me until I die: my Glasgow, my native city, my blessing, my curse, my great love and my pet hate, my dream place and my nightmare, my green and grimy city, my essential home place, my constant contradiction. Even its coat of arms displays a paradox:

Here's the tree that never grew,
Here's the bird that never flew,
Here's the fish that never swam,
Here's the bell that never rang.

That's Glasgow: awkward from the start. The word 'Glasgow' itself is Gaelic from *Glas cu*, and it means 'grey dog' or 'gray rock', but to most Glaswegians, it's just 'Glesca', the 'dear green place'. But it is not just a place, it's a state of mind. I can close my eyes and I see green – a 'dear green place' in all its unexpectedness. How can any conjunction of stone and steel, concrete and asphalt, brick and plaster, wood and plastic, remain so fixed in the mind as a thing of beauty? Because it *is* beautiful. Not pretty or nice or pleasant, but deeply beautiful, like an older woman who has eschewed lipstick and powder for something indefinable in the eyes. That's my Glasgow: four thousand years old, but she still has that certain something.

So, if we're going to talk about her, I'd better introduce her properly. Assuming that, like ships, all cities are female, then just like any woman, each has its own distinctive personality. If London is the world's dowager queen mother, Paris is its wicked aunt and New York is everybody's boisterous cousin. Rome is the next-door neighbour who takes in priests as lodgers. Glasgow has no pretensions to this first circle of great cities, unlike the status-conscious Edinburgh, but it is moving up fast in world ratings all the same, because Glasgow has recently discovered 'style' and is making it all her own.

It has taken over from Liverpool as the first city of pop, a veritable 'Oasis' for bands, and there isn't a pop fan anywhere who doesn't know that a former Rector of Glasgow University is Jim Kerr of Simple Minds. An association that doesn't immediately come to mind, but one has to remember that Glasgow is the least Scottish of Scotland's cities. In fact, it owes more in personality to Chicago than anywhere else; but the new boutique Glasgow, following hard on the recent Charles Rennie Mackintosh renaissance, is selling its own kind of modern cheeky-chic creativity. 'You know but' is cool, and 'Jimmy' has entered the language as an endearment, but the place itself, even if it is becoming a tourist Mecca, is still not entirely 'respectable'.

The first thing to be said about Glasgow is that she is no lady. She talks too loudly and laughs too readily. Not like her big sister, Edinburgh, who knows how to behave on every occasion. Being older than Glasgow, Edinburgh had to stay at home and look after her old fatherland. She had more than one chance to marry, especially over the border, but never did. She knew where her duty lay. So, with pursed lips and nose held high, she carried on, smug in the knowledge that she was doing the right thing, and she made sure everybody knew it.

Glasgow, on the other hand, was always wild and caused her mother-country a lot of worry when growing up. She could never keep her face clean, yet she never lacked for admirers. She had a child out of wedlock, called Dundee (they say the father was an Irishman), and Glasgow had to leave home. She went for a time to relatives in Belfast but soon came back to set up her own place. There are still strong family links with Ireland. Glasgow's second cousin, Dublin, used to be close but there's been an estrangement there. Dublin and Belfast have been bitter for years so the rest of the family won't visit. They don't want to take sides. It's very sad. But that's families.

According to Edinburgh, Glasgow is a disgrace to the family. But Glasgow doesn't mind: she doesn't *need* Edinburgh, which always annoys that superior place. However, Glasgow gets on well with her cheeky offspring, Dundee, who has just the same sort of spirit as Glasgow, whom she idolizes. Dundee would have liked to have been another Glasgow but never had that lady's nerve. Dundee has her own style all the same and she doesn't talk to Edinburgh either.

Perth, who is Dundee's posh auntie, hates living so near this little Glasgow-on the-Dee and would rather live nearer Edinburgh. Just as Dundee idolizes Glasgow, Perth worships Edinburgh. She sees in her oldest sister all that she would liked to have been herself, but although she had the looks and the breeding, she hadn't the inner steel of the born leader and is glad to leave all the decisions to the top girl in the family. Stirling was Perth's twin, but not of the identical sort. They get on well enough but Stirling, being born first, is the stronger and always felt she should have been a boy. She is the only one who is not afraid to stand up to either Glasgow or Edinburgh and considers that *she* should be the natural capital of the country anyway. She is centrally-placed and has her own castle, ready-made for the new Scottish Parliament – and just think what that would have saved in time, money and bewilderment.

There is no doubt that Stirling has a case for being Scotland's Second City, but she is too sensible to press the possibility too hard. She knows when she is well off. She has a comfortable home, a lovely garden and none of the worries of her older sisters, so she gets on quietly with her own thing. Aberdeen is much the same. She was swept off her feet by a rich American while she was still at school and is quite happy well away from the rest of the family, counting her money and waiting for the day she can move to Texas where all her real friends are. Inverness, the baby of the family, was a late child, quite unexpected, and rumour has it that the real father had royal connections, but they don't talk about that in correct circles: the feeling there is that if nothing is said then nothing ever happened.

Like all families, the Scottish sisterhood of cities has had its ups and downs over the years, but they're still there. With their various offspring, Dumfries and Kilmarnock in the west, Kirkcaldy and Dunfermline in the east, not to mention the new generation already growing up in the five grandchildren new towns – Livingston, Glenrothes, Cumbernauld, East Kilbride and Irvine – there's room for a few surprises yet. But, honestly, I can't see Edinburgh ever going west. Unless, that is, Glasgow decides to elope to Chicago.

Which Glasgow would never do, because she's wedded to her river. She is a river city and has lived on and off the waters of the Clyde from the time the river rose out of the Leadhills in Lanarkshire and made its way through the infant Glasgow to the sea. This waterway was a vital element in the emerging township and proved a decisive factor in its growth. It still runs broad and deep through its centre following the sun west to the Tail o' the Bank and the Atlantic Ocean. Glasgow has always looked westward to the Americas, just as Edinburgh has always looked east towards Europe. Like Liverpool, Glasgow made its fortune in transatlantic trade, but it chose tobacco and cotton rather than that human cargo imported from West Africa. This didn't make the Glasgow commercial barons any better than their English counterparts; merely different.

Glasgow is the largest city in Scotland and ideally situated to be recognised as Scotland's chief commercial centre, for it stands astride its river and looks out to sea and the rest of the world. It's been doing that since it was a tiny fording place on the banks of the River Clyde, and went on doing so when it became a great trading post, and then an international seaport and finally an industrial metropolis. It was once the Second City of the Empire, but that empire is now long gone, as are the industries. However, Glasgow has struck back and is rapidly emerging as a tourist attraction, an international arts centre, and the true cultural capital of Scotland.

It's hard to believe now that it first achieved fame as a beauty spot. As early as 1650, proceedings in Parliament drew the happy comment: 'The town of Glasgow, though not so big, nor so rich, yet to all seems a much sweeter and more delightful place than Edinburgh.' Who can disagree with that? Samuel Pepys came north in 1682 as part of the train of the Duke of York (the later King James VI and I) and found Glasgow to be 'a very extraordinary town for beauty and trade, much superior to any in Scotland.' But Pepys found the people much less attractive. He had 'a dislike of their personal habits... a rooted nastiness hangs about the person of every Scot (man and woman).' Only a Londoner could say a thing like that.

Daniel Defoe was much more flattering, but then he was an English Dissenter and came to Glasgow straight from prison in 1726. He called the town 'the emporium of Scotland... stately and well-built, standing on a plain in a manner four square... it is one of the most beautiful places in the country.' Defoe came back several times, which is a compliment to any place. He was also one of the first to see the possibilities in a Forth and Clyde Canal. Defoe had a sharp eye, an advantage to any spy. By 1770, Tobias Smollett, a Dumbarton man, could also see the possibilities in Glasgow, referring to it as 'the pride of Scotland, which might pass for a flourishing city in any part of Christendom.'

Scotland's National Bard, Robert Burns, made five visits to Glasgow between 1787 and 1791, on book business with John Smith in St Vincent Place and always stayed at Duthie's Black Bull Inn in Argyle Street. From there he wrote to his Edinburgh *amour* of the time, 'Clarinda', who was actually a Glasgow girl, Nancy McLehose née Craig, the daughter of a Glasgow surgeon from the Saltmarket. Burns met up with Captain Richard Brown in Glasgow for 'one of the happiest occasions of my life' – meaning they both got very drunk. It was Brown, a sailor, who had earlier given Burns the idea of becoming 'a poet in print', so we have much to be grateful to Captain Brown for. Betty, Burns' illegitimate daughter to Anna Park of the Globe Inn in Dumfries, grew up to marry a soldier and settled down in Pollokshaws. Following the poet's death in

1796, Betty received £200 from the fund set up for the Burns family. This was the poet's only gesture towards Glasgow.

Another poet, William Wordsworth, came to Glasgow in 1803 with his sister, Dorothy, and good friend and fellow-poet, Samuel Coleridge. They were on their way to pay their respects to Burns' grave in Dumfries and visit his Cottage in Ayr. In Glasgow, they stayed at the Saracen's Head in the Gallowgate, but neither poet was inspired to write anything about the city, though Dorothy did note in her journal that 'the streets were as handsome as streets can be'. JJ Audubon, the American ornithologist, arrived in 1829 with copies of his famous book of birds but only managed to sell one copy, and that was to the Hunterian Museum at the University. Mr Audubon was not impressed by Glasgow's apathy to American birds.

William Thackeray, in Glasgow to give a series of lectures in 1852, was another who did not take to the city: 'What a hideous, smoking Babel it is, after the clear, London atmosphere, quite unbearable.' He also took exception to the large number of what he called 'Hirishmen' he heard in the streets, no more than many Scots themselves did. Nor was Charles Dickens a Glasgow admirer. He read from his works there in 1861 and 1868, but thought it 'a dreadful place'. He also added that 'it rains as it never does rain anywhere else.' Did he mean that the rain went *up*?

It is interesting to note the graph of disparagement grow as Glasgow developed from the almost sylvan seventeenth and eighteenth centuries to the industrial effects of furnaces and smoking chimneys in the nineteenth. Even the statues turned ebony black in the atmosphere. This actually improved many of them, but goodness knows what it did to living lungs. That not so eminent Victorian poet, William McGonagall, came to Glasgow from Dundee to be entertained by a group of University students at a banquet in Dennistoun. After much mock-ceremony, he was duly dubbed by them Sir William 'Topaz' McGonagall, Knight of the White Elephant of Burma – and awarded the status of the best worst poet in the world. The irrepressible McGonagall was not deterred. He knew he would be remembered. And he was right; he is genuinely famous for failing, which is perhaps what Glasgow liked about him. What we do know is that he liked Glasgow:

O, beautiful City of Glasgow
That stands on the River Clyde,

How happy should the people be
That in you reside.
For you are the most enterprising city
Of the present day
Whatever anybody else might say.

It was all too good to last, and it didn't. By McGonagall's time, heavy industries had encroached on the green place, and it was hard to see the town for smoke. It was no longer picturesque. Every street seemed to sprout a factory chimney, or 'chimley' as the natives called it, and every tenement contributed its noxious mix to the deadly canopy that hung over everything and everyone. What had been genuinely picturesque so recently was gradually enveloped in soot, grime and engine oil, each of them conspiring to disfigure old, grey stones that had stood since the Romans. However, plenty of lovely money was being made by some out of the unsightly conditions, and the mercantile princes of plunder made mansions for themselves along the Great Western Road – which might as well have been called the Great Gatsby Road such was its splendour. In 1889, the Doge of Venice's Palace was recreated by William Lieper on Glasgow Green as a carpet factory for Mr Templeton. This was Glasgow hubris at its best – or worst – but when it wanted the best, it got it.

If the nineteenth century was good for the Glasgow businessman, it wasn't so good for the ordinary Glaswegian who was paying dearly for trade expansion and prosperity. The incoming Highland and Irish migrants, who had flooded into the city to escape either absentee English landlords or the potato famine, were crowded into the new tenements like herring in a box. New tenements were sprouting up all over the inner city, trying to keep up with a population that seemed to be growing by the hour. Glasgow was gradually evolving its own kind of people, and most of them were below the poverty line. Many died early among the muddy streets, running drains and damp walls. In order to survive at all, they had to develop a close neighbourliness against their common plight, a spirited defiance of their living condition. This is how they gained the term 'gallus', a kind of *esprit de la rue,* a streetwise insouciance, which Glaswegians have retained to this day, marking them out from all other Scots – especially those in Edinburgh.

Unlike the 'Edin-buggers', the Glasgow proletariat has no great history to speak of, and the eastern bloc rather looked down on the western bloke. It still does. Everyone looks down on the Glaswegian for he is generally smaller than most. The city's old regiment, the Glasgow Light Infantry, formerly out of Maryhill Barracks (now a shopping mall), were Glasgow's own Ghurkas, and just as fearsome in their bantam way. Have you noticed that all our boxing champions, from Benny Lynch to Jim Watt, were lightweights? Nonetheless, they weigh heavily in terms of Glasgow's regard for their own. They don't need Edinburgh's cobwebbed ghosts.

Thomas Moore in his lovely song, *Believe Me If All Those Endearing Young Charms,* tells us that 'the sunflower turns on her god, when he sets, the same look which she turned when he rose'. This meteorological balance doesn't seem to apply along the M8 motorway linking Glasgow and Edinburgh. Or is it that there is just a lack of sunflowers in Lowland Scotland? Since the sun is the source of all living things, there may be a co-relation between the effects of the sun's rising or setting on the character and personality of those who see it first and those who see it last. At any rate, east is still east but west is best – for some of us. This westward demographic inclination was just as evident in ancient times. If the Persians looked west to Egypt, the Greeks did likewise across the Ionian Sea to where the Italian coast lay just over the horizon. To them it was the edge of the world with the Great Unknown beyond it. What was there, in fact, were the Roman legions and by the beginning of Christendom it was they who ended nearly a thousand years of Hellenistic sway.

Roman power and influence spread over the whole known world of that time before its sceptre went west again into the hands of the Germanic Charlemagne, who became the first Holy Roman Emperor of the West by 800AD. It was the Teutons, moving west once more, who gave the Roman Londinium its Celtic name, London, at a time when Arthur's Seat was still vacant and Dunedin was little more than the rock it stood on. Glasgow was then no more than a wee green spot on the banks of the Molendinar Burn where it trickled into the Clyde. All this is discoverable fact borne out by history, but if a similar westward instinct thus should ever manifest itself in Scotland during the second millennium then it is quite possible that the capital itself might move west to Glasgow.

Changing the capital of a country is not a new idea: once upon a time, Dunfermline ruled in Scotland, so did Stirling. It's almost accepted today that in any country there are two capitals, one official and one actual. We know that in the United States the talking is done in Washington but the action takes place in New York. The same applies to Ottawa and Toronto in Canada – with Quebec having nothing to do with either of them. Similarly, Germany has Bonn and Berlin, while Russia has Moscow and St Petersburg. Most countries have a working city and a showplace city, a weekday capital and a Sunday one. Except in England, where London, arguably the most famous city in the world, is still the capital and hub of the country, if not of the whole British Isles. Paris comes a close second, although you don't say so in France. To the French, Paris is the capital of the world.

The point is that this division of purpose, the separation of function into the executive and the consultative, is perhaps not such a bad thing. By each playing to its strength, they minimise their respective weaknesses. Parliament works this way with the House of Lords as does the US Senate with Congress – or at least they try to. The same applies to Anglo-Saxon Edinburgh and Celtic Glasgow, the prim office and the untidy factory, the front room and the kitchen – sharing the same house but not speaking. So near and yet so far. What kind of country would Scotland be if we swapped things round so that Glasgow became the capital and Edinburgh the workplace? It would be a lot more fun for one thing. Except that we would never get anything done. Edinburgh would go in a huff and Glasgow would probably bankrupt the nation by holding a citywide party to celebrate its new status. Nevertheless, a combination of Glasgow's zest and Edinburgh's class would make a formidable capital. Perhaps it could be situated near the middle of the M8. They could call it Shottsville – or *Bathgate Brazilia? Nae borra.* No, on second thoughts, it might be wiser to leave well alone and keep things as they are.

'Suit yersel,' as the wee man said.

CHAPTER ONE

Bullish Beginnings

THE BULL STOPS HERE

EVERYONE BELONGS TO somewhere and I belong to Glasgow. I am only one of that myriad of mongrel ingredients that have gone into Glasgow's ethnic make-up over the last four thousand years. The demographics involved are colourful to say the least, but this very lack of pedigree might explain the city's particular vitality and exuberance. The city's aboriginals, after all, had painted faces and a fierce fighting tradition – so what's changed? The Celts, (pronounced with a 'K') emerged from the Albanian mountains in the early morning of civilization and moved up through its young days via Morocco, Spain, Brittany, Cornwall and Wales and the Lake District before arriving in North Britain in what is now the Lowland West of Scotland at a point then called Cathures, where the Molendinar Burn runs into the Clyde.

Pursuing them all the way were the Romans, those proto-Italians, who, under orders from Emperor Antoninus Pius, got as far as the outskirts of Old Kilpatrick before being beaten back by the midges, that very underrated last line of defence for all who live beyond Hadrian's

Wall. The ferocious Celts forced the Romans to build the Antonine Wall, to help keep the natives (and the midges) out. Because of their painted faces, the Romans dubbed these spunky people the Picts, and their descendants can still be seen strutting the streets of Glasgow today. Inner city types; bantam, lithe, dark-haired men who don't paint their faces but often bring a blush to other people's.

The mass exodus of the Romans after nearly five hundred years left the way clear for the next invaders, the Gaelic-speaking Scots from Ulster led by King Fergus in 503AD. These Scots who had already been converted to Christianity by St Columba of Iona, overcame the Britonnic Celts of Strathclyde, and finally settled in Dalriada, an area in Kintyre first mapped out by St Ninian. It could be defined more or less as the region containing the city of Glasgow and its surrounding environs. Ninian's culture in the east of Scotland had produced *The Goddodin* of Teutonic Edinburgh which was the basic source for the Arthurian legend. Who knows, King Arthur might have been a North Briton? After all, Arthur's Seat is right in the city centre. While St Cuthbert looked for other Angles to bring Christianity to the region around the Forth, the Picts, under King Brude, moved north and operated north of the Forth and Clyde mainly out of their fort in Inverness.

This then was the state of sixth-century Scotland when Fergus died in 525 at Culross Abbey. One of the monks there, Kentigern, was instructed to harness a bull to a cart and place the body in it. He was then to bury the king wherever the bull stopped. It was hardly a papal bull, but it was an order and Kentigern dutifully complied. Both the monk and the bull must have had stamina because they walked fifty miles or so across lowland Scotland before coming to a halt at Cathures, the Celtic settlement on the Clyde. Here St Ninian had already prepared a graveyard so Kentigern duly installed Fergus as its first client, and himself as its first priest. There is no record of what happened to the bull.

Tradition tells us that Kentigern was the illegitimate son of a princess, who had been cast out to sea in an open boat by her father when he found out she was pregnant. In his anger and shame he left her to the mercy of the elements, which washed her up at the Culross monastery on the shores of the Forth. The monks took her in and later trained her boy Kentigern for the priesthood. This was the boy who became the man, Mungo, who eventually became Glasgow's patron saint and a figure on its coat of arms together with the bird, the bell, the tree and the fish.

Each of these symbols is linked to the miracles Mungo is reputed to have worked in his life of more than one hundred years. He predicated that a lost ring would be found in a salmon's mouth. It was presumably a freshwater fish, but this sort of legend has to be taken with a pinch of salt. Another involved a hill that rose under him as he preached, while yet another told of the branch he had broken off from a tree that would burst into flames at his touch so that he could light a fire. There is no reason given why the bell never rang except that it might have just lost its tongue. Legends like these last for all sorts of reasons, none of which need be true.

Meantime, young Glasgow was stretching through her green years taking in and taking on various strains and septs that attended the line of Scottish kings stumbling through the Dark Ages. Normans, Saxons, Angles and Danes were all racial stages up to and including the fourteenth-century Robert the Bruce, who was really French but spoke conversational Latin. Three hundred years later the Continental connection was maintained by Bonnie Prince Charlie, who brought his rabble of Highlanders down to accept the quiet surrender of Glasgow to the Jacobites in 1745. The prince and his tartan army encamped at Shawfield and made as good a show on Glasgow Green as ever the carnival was later to do during the Glasgow Fair.

Not every Highlander came south waving a claymore. Some were not even Jacobite and it was the more sober, God-fearing Presbyterian Highland scholar who now walked the twisting miles from the north. He was to leave his inky imprint not only in Glasgow but all over the world as the archetypal classroom dominie. Little more than boys themselves, they brought their Bibles and their bags of oats to the university and from there graduated to become indispensable cogs in the education machine. Every Glasgow school had its Highland teacher, usually in the English Department, specialising in the Classics, imposing his severe standards on generations of little town tikes who 'crept unwillingly' to listen to precisely enunciated knowledge imparted in tones that made everything sound like a sermon. The late, great, comic actor Duncan Macrae was such a teacher, and Roddy MacMillan, also a fine Glasgow actor in recent times, and a fellow-Highlander, was one of his pupils in Anderston.

It was from this same Highland stock that a good proportion of Glasgow's future population came, and at least half of its intimidating police force. A new clan of constables emerged throughout the twentieth century, each as tall as a pine tree, and often just as thick, but offering a police image that was daunting. Just imagine an arboreal giant in heavy boots and large helmet charging at you, baton in hand. You never saw his eyes under the helmet. Perhaps he didn't have any to speak of, which was why he blindly followed orders to the letter. Still, the big Highland bobby was an unmissable feature of street life in Glasgow until the 'Z-car' sixties, and he kept those same streets as clean as the Corporation Cleansing Department ever did.

The Gaelic Glaswegian gave us words like 'glaikit' from *gliogaid* and 'skelp' from the Gaelic *sgealp*. However, the most used Gaelic word in Glasgow appears to be 'ach' or 'och', which Glaswegians have adopted as their own. While gregarious Glasgow didn't adopt the Highland clan system, it developed its own style of street co-operative, which was more or less the same thing, but with smoke and soot in place of Scotch mist. The tartan territory was the above-mentioned Anderston, which was about as far south as the Highlanders went in the city. Here they built their own community with its own Highland Hall near the once beautiful Charing Cross, but the main social centre for the Northerners was the Hielandman's Umbrella. This was the Central Station's railway bridge over Argyle Street where the 'tcheuchters', as the other Glaswegians familiarly called them, could shelter from the rain and hear news from home. Highlanders rarely ventured to the east or south of the city.

It was to the south that the Jews came. It was only when many of that old race moved from Holland and Germany towards the end of the eighteenth century that Glasgow could be said to get down to business. The Jews originally settled in Edinburgh but it did not take them long to see the error of their ways and they soon made their way west. One can see the development of these intrepid pioneers in terms of their synagogues and burial grounds, both of which became larger with each generation. It was the end of the nineteenth century which saw the next Jewish surge when the incomers arrived direct from Poland and Russia and settled in the Gorbals. Shops were opened and cash registers chimed as fortunes were founded on hard graft done at the counter and the cutting room. What is called the 'rag-trade' grew out of the rags that many of these specialist tailors and garment workers had arrived in.

They did not stay ragged long. Money spoke louder than Yiddish and this new status allowed the Jewish community to make a formidable input into the life of Glasgow, especially its culture. This Jewish flavour has been a very valuable and exotic ingredient to the Glasgow mix, and the city continues to benefit from it, as do many countries far removed from Israel. It is largely thanks to its Jewish population that Glasgow still has its theatres. Jewish involvement via the Goldberg family, especially Michael Goldberg, made possible the development of the Citizens' Theatre from playwright James Bridie's embryo at the Athenaeum to a civic playhouse now enjoying an international standing.

The Goldbergs were also behind every second art gallery in the West End. They are typical in recent times of the enlightened Jewish contribution to the arts in the city. Sir Isaac Wolfson has also played his part by donating major benefactions to Glasgow University and his name graces a whole new campus on the north side of the city. Dr Benno Schotz, the Queen's Sculptor in Scotland, was a Jew who came to Glasgow by way of Estonia in 1914, and rose to own a studio/mansion in Kirklee at the Botanic Gardens. Benno brought his east European *elan* to a Glasgow that was ready-made for him. He had come through pogroms and exile to get there but he could now laugh it all off. The best thing he had done, he always said, was to come to 'Schotz-land' as he called it, and to 'Class-co', which he said he loved for its 'brio'.

In 1968 I sat for him for a bust as Robert Burns. I was given, at the same time, extra-mural tuition in the arts just listening to him talk. I was clay in his hands, in every sense. When I look at the bronze today it's his twinkling face I see. He phoned me at my mother's flat in Dennistoun on his 92nd birthday and chuckled into my ear, 'I thought the Lord would take me in the night. I asked Him to, but He didn't listen to me, so I have a whole day I didn't expect. What am I going to do with it?' Benno, with his Glasgow-Estonian zest, made it seem as if he'd been given a huge bonus of a fresh day – at 92. All he wanted to do by then was join his wife, Millie, who had been in Abraham's bosom for some time, but as long as he had breath, he had life and he filled his day. As it happened, he went to his Millie not long afterwards, so God must have been listening after all.

Beryl Cutler was our Jewish doctor in Parkhead. He was also a Hebrew scholar specialising in Jewish pre-history. Beryl did not live as long as Benno but he packed a lot into his day-job serving the poor Irish for pennies in post-war Parkhead. Between calls, he went back to his books like Faustus. In his study he was trying to fathom the complexities of ancient man in the Middle East, and in his surgery he was doing much the same with his patients in the East End. Whenever I went to collect medicine for my mother or father, Dr Cutler would always discuss what I was reading at the time before signing another prescription. When I later went to university, I used to see him in the Reading Room on his day off, though I could never see much of him as he was always half-hidden behind a large pile of books.

When he made a house call at Williamson Street during my father's last illness, I would hear them discussing Martin Buber and Kierkegaard in the kitchen and debating, sometimes heatedly, the idea of Man's direct relationship with God. I remember my mother was quite impatient with these debates. She wasn't into religious existentialism. A quick 'Hail Mary' did it for her. All she wanted to know was if my father's blood count or pulse rate was up or down, but Beryl Cutler attended the mind as well as the body. He knew that was the healthier part of my father. I can't remember much of their conversations but I do remember their laughter. Beryl Cutler wasn't a big man but his mind was huge by any standards and he gave of it gladly to anyone interested. And he did so with laughter. He knew its importance.

No one knew that better than the Irish, the next insurgent wave to surge across Glasgow, except that they didn't have much to laugh about. Their mid-to-late nineteenth-century advent was their second coming as it were, and it was mainly due to the failure of the potato crop in 1845. *An Gorta Mor*, or the Great Hunger, drove thousands from their farms and on to the boats that sent the Irish around the world. Those with money went to Australia, those with some savings bought a passage to America, but those with nothing but the clothes they stood up in, scraped fourpence together to cross, standing-room only, in the cattle-boats to Liverpool and Glasgow.

The Glasgow 'paddies' came from tilling the sod in Down and Donegal to toiling under it in the Lanarkshire coal mines, but they were glad to get the work. In time, they created a lot of little Irelands all over the city and its environs, from Garngad down to the Gorbals, spilling over the eastern boundaries into places like Holytown, Carfin, Coatbridge and Baillieston. It was this last area which took in the Kearneys, McKerneys and Carneys, as the Cairneys were variously called, depending on the Registrar of Birth's hearing. Irish-Glaswegians even created their own Cathedral. St Andrew's is on the banks of the Clyde in the centre of the city not so far from the ford where St Mungo had served the first settlers, the ancient Celtic Catholics. Later Catholics, almost up to recent times, had always to build their church or school in a side street. They could not be seen to be prominent on any main thoroughfare.

However, the Irish were survivors, and they hung in there, putting their trust in God and the Celtic Football Club to maintain their spiritual and temporal welfare. The combination must have worked, for as well as supplying footballers to Celtic, they have made up most of Glasgow's local politicians to this day, introducing a touch of Tamanay Hall to the Council Chambers. A system of favours was introduced where nothing was said, certainly nothing was put in writing, but things were done on a nod and a wink and the clink of a glass. There was much scratching of backs, but no blood was ever drawn. As long as you knew, of course, that a quiet 'no' sometimes meant 'yes'. That's how Irish the system was. Nevertheless, the strain produced men of the calibre of Professor James Brogan of Brains Trust fame, as well as Jimmy Boyle, the hooligan turned sculptor; Lord Jimmy Gordon of Radio Clyde; Dr Gerald McGrath, the former optician and City Baillie, who today carries his St Mungo's Academy French and German into Europe's inner circles; and the 'Great Defender' Len Murray, from the same school, who made his orator's name in the law courts and at Burns Suppers. Glasgow entertainers of Irish extraction are almost taken for granted, but Glen Daly, Matt McGinn and Billy Connolly come to mind. Pre-war tenor Canon Sidney McEwan seemed to have the best of both worlds, secular and spiritual. That's what they call the luck of the Irish.

The end of the nineteenth century brought more Catholics, but they were of the Italian variety. All Italians are good Catholics until their mothers die and then they catch up on the secular life with a healthy gusto. The first Italians to arrive in any numbers since the Romans were master-stonemasons. They came over with the late-Victorian army of craftsmen to build the figured marble halls that were to become the Glasgow City Chambers. The Carrara marble of its interior still makes the visitor gasp as much as the original city councillors did at the cost. However, it was well worth it and those Italian hands stamped with their artistry the confidence the city then felt in itself and in its citizens.

With the building done, most of the craftsmen stayed on in Glasgow to sell home-made ice cream from a coloured cart on the street. They spoke little English, but neither did many of their customers. Most Italian immigrants learned the language from their street trading. As a result, many of them could swear before they could converse, but when they were lost for words they would sing loudly in Italian which delighted the urchin onlookers. Italians were always likeable and outgoing and they quickly blended in to become vivid and viable Glaswegians. They showed no great interest in politics or football but a connection was made with the latter in 1966 with the arrival of Lou Macari at Celtic FC.

Another Italian to make his mark in Glasgow was the architect Jack Coia, with his individual churches. His seminary at Cardross has won heritage status for its design. His namesake, but no relation, Emilio Coia, the art critic and cartoonist, became a pillar of the Glasgow Arts Club on Bath Street. All these men would have known the Italian Centre in Ingram Street which exists today almost in the shadow of the City Chambers which their forebears had helped to build. Interestingly, their Glasgow descendants have reversed the trend by buying up properties in Italy and there are walled streets in Lucca, Braga and San Gimignano that echo to the whine of familiar Glasgow voices, trying hard to convince the locals that they are also Italians. *That's right, Jimmy, we're Tallies tae. Pit it there, pal. Great. See's a wee spaghetti an' a pint a that Chianti. OK? Brilliant.*

The first black family I ever saw in Parkhead were called London and they lived on Glamis Road. They were handsome Jamaican and the father looked just like Harry Belafonte. They were the first coloured people seen in our peely-wally neighbourhood which only saw colour on match days, but they were not to be the last. The Ugandan Indians arrived thanks to the cruelties of Idi Amin, then came the Hindus and Sikhs, followed by the Pakistanis. A veritable flood as wide as the Ganges flowed into the Clyde. It was certainly a bigger infusion than the Molendinar Burn had ever been.

The first effect of this influx throughout the sixties and seventies was the loss of the wee 'Jenny a' thing' shop on the corner and the disappearance of local dairy as we knew it. This soon re-emerged as the ubiquitous 'Paki's', which proved just as handy. Turbanned bus drivers became the thing as the driving licence took the place of the peddler's licence for much of the Asian community and before long the Sikh had swapped his bicycle and suitcase for a van. There is no possibility, however, that he will ever exchange his sacred knife for a Glasgow razor. These are different men in a different day. A prosperous, commercial Indian enclave soon developed around North Woodlands Road and Charing Cross and a parked BMW at the pavement set the seal on hard work and initiative by whole families.

The indigenous Glaswegian, whoever he was by now, embraced the new citizenry as much as he had accepted every other arrival and retreated to the safety of his settee to watch Rab C. Nesbitt on television. The difference was skin colour. The new Glaswegians stood out because of it, in a way that the Irish, Jews and Italians had not. A Chinaman couldn't very well pretend to be other than a Chinaman. Why should he? A man's a man an' a' that. It was as plain as black and white and brown came somewhere in the middle. It was a fact of modern life and had to be dealt with. It wasn't a problem, it was a situation, and Glasgow, the seaport that had seen it all, took it all on board and quite unselfconsciously flaunted its coat of many colours.

The fact is that Glasgow is multi-racial but not multi-ghetto. The ethnic groups that washed by the banks of the Clyde over the centuries didn't take long to move out of their original campsites within the city and swim in the mainstream as it were. A nucleus was retained of the old bridgeheads, in that the Irish kept a hold in the east and the Highlanders in the west. The Jews were mainly in the south but the gregarious Italians were everywhere. The Indian races stayed at the centre, and fanned out only to serve their upward and outward spiral of little businesses. The Chinese favoured the old dock areas but were happy to go where there was money to be made. All this glorious maelstrom of peoples, busy doing their thing, was largely ignored by the native Glaswegian. His 'couldn't care less' attitude was accepted as tolerance, but what did it matter, it has come out all right in the end, more or less. The truth is, the basic division of Glasgow is still religious rather than ethnic, at least as the ordinary man in the street sees it.

The Protestant ascendancy of mostly professional people still stood in the divided city faced by the threat of the Catholic 'hired hands' with all the others as neutrals scuttling uneasily between the two impenetrable cliff-faces. This simplistic view recognised the apartheid that already existed in education and job opportunities and it would take more than fashionable political correctness to cure the gnarled mistrust between the two factions that is so deep-rooted in the city's consciousness. Given this attitude, there was no welcome assimilation of all the new races; there was only apathy. What did it matter who came to Glasgow? What would change? The twin pillars of bigotry would still stand, even if they were only sustained by the existence of a couple of professional football clubs. Celtic and Rangers have more to answer for than their results on a Saturday, but this is a huge question in itself and is dealt with elsewhere in this book. For the moment we must confine ourselves to the other racial ingredients that make up the multi-coloured city which Glasgow has now become.

Schisms thrive in a ghetto climate, as we saw at Notting Hill Gate in 1968 and more recently in Manchester and Birmingham, but Glasgow has been free of such racial confrontations so far as she didn't resist or openly resent the incursion of her coloured citizens. The late Enoch Powell's dire warnings of 'rivers of blood' between Hindu and Muslim or blacks and their white neighbours never happened on the Clyde, because the Clydesiders, with typical *sang-froid*, just let them all come. And even if it was absorption by indifference, there are worse ways.

St Mungo had prophesied all those centuries ago that Glasgow would flourish by the preaching of the Word but I doubt he expected that it would be in Urdu or Cantonese. Or that the kirks and chapels would give way to mosques and temples. This is Glasgow with a difference and it's the differences that make it what is today: a cosmopolitan, international city in every sense of the word. Yet for all these surface differences, it's still *homo sapiens* underneath. We're all soup from the same stock, whether it was Jock Tamson or Old Adam, and however we have ended up, we're all as God made us – God help us. As the man said, 'It takes a' kinds'. But in Glasgow he would be sure to add, 'Aye, that'll be right'.

That same wee man has somehow retained an essential optimism. He needed to and even his pub songs reflected this unquenchable hope for the best:

> For I'm fu' the noo,
> Absolutely fu',
> An' I adore the country I was born in.
> My name is Jock McGraw
> An' I dinnae care a straw,
> For I've a wee drop in the bottle for the mornin'.

So he makes his unsteady way down the long corridor of his city's history, often stumbling, sometimes running or sliding and slipping, but doggedly keeping going, edging his way through it all until he stands before us now in all his glory.

See him in his modern mode: a tartan turban showing a glimpse of a trendy haircut, a white silk Indian scarf thrown casually over his Armani tracksuit (which has been specially designed with a chip on each shoulder). We get a glimpse of his T-shirt, which was made in China and he stands as tall as he can in his Taiwan trainers. A sprig of heather is in one lapel, a shamrock in the other and the Star of David is worn on his sleeve. This is the sartorial amalgam that symbolises mongrel Glasgow in its best sense but the Glaswegian still gives it to you, straight, and in your face:

> *'Sfunny, in't it? Know what I mean? 'Safact, but. Nae hee-haw. Naw, I mean, it's hist'ry, n'that. Loada shite, by the way. Know what I mean?*

It's an attitude which stems from a long way back, a view formed by vicissitude and hardened by painful experience but underpinned by an atavistic optimism which is his strongest weapon and his safest shield: 'We've never died a winter yet,' he'll boast. So he soldiers on towards his future, whatever it entails. And, as he goes, hear him still singing out cheerfully,

> O, we're no' awa' tae bide awa'
> We're no' awa' tae leave ye,
> We're no' awa' tae bide awa,
> We'll ay come back an' see ye.

And that's his threat. Although he might go away for a time, he'll always come back, as perky and indomitable as ever. This Celtiberian is a survivor and however much the road ahead twists and turns, he will twist and turn with it until he ends up where he's supposed to be. Which might indeed be the very place he started out from – deep in the heart of Glasgow.

CHAPTER TWO

A Transport of Delight

THREE INTO ONE WON'T GO

IF NEW YORK IS THE Big Apple, what then is Glasgow? If by their fruits
ye shall know them, what else could she be but a Honey Pear? Bruised
and discoloured here and there perhaps, and not to everyone's taste, but
it's one that grows on you. The fruitful analogy also comes to mind when
you consider Glasgow's Clockwork Orange, the Lilliputian subway
service, so called because of the unique colour of its rolling stock. These
dinky little trains go happily round and round in concentric circles to the
delight of non-claustrophobic citizens, who are inured to stale air.
Getting on and off its toy-like carriages is a daily game played under the
Glasgow streets by passengers who hop on and off between Partick and
St George's Cross, Govan and St Enoch's Square in order to get to all
points north, south, east and west of the city centre.

There is talk of extending its radius. That would be good but I hope
they don't change the colour. A yellow Jaffa wouldn't be the same
somehow. Vivid orange is the perfect colour to emerge from a black
tunnel. Being at the very core of Glasgow, the Orange peels off to

everywhere. With its links to the district lines and the main railway terminals it also means that any destination is possible. You could get on the subway at Cowcaddens and finish up in Tashkent if you wanted to. It's all a matter of connections. The only problem is where to start.

In the older Glasgow the first thing you did when you wanted to go anywhere was to walk to the nearest tram stop. Unless you were really flash and took a taxi, and even then it would just be to get to the closest tram stop. Everything in that other Glasgow began and ended at the tram stop. Shakespeare's Puck said he would 'put a girdle round the earth in forty minutes'. A tram might have taken a bit longer to get round the whole of Glasgow, but, given a change of car here and there, you could do it – and all for little more than a few pennies. Again, it was a matter of connections. Public transport was more than a utility for Glaswegians of that era; it was a way of life.

Pre-tram, the proletariat walked and the gentry went by horse and carriage, and later by horse-drawn omnibus. However, when the railed car arrived, all social levels seemed to take advantage of the new electric traction method, because it was so very convenient. The tram was a German/American development during the nineteenth century and one of its inventors was a man who was Daft – Leo Daft. He didn't quite live up to his name, for his system was taken up in 1860 by another American, appropriately called Train. Mr Train brought the idea to London and ten years later, when Parliament gave the go-ahead to local authorities to install their own tram systems, one John Young brought the tram system to Glasgow as a basis for interurban and suburban travel.

Soon, the Glasgow tramways system was a showcase to the world. This was due entirely to the vision of a Galloway man called James Dalrymple. As General Manager of the Glasgow Corporation Tramways Department, he took over from John Young at a time when the first tramcars were drawn by horses, but his name soon became synonymous with transport in Glasgow. In 1894, he oversaw the embedding of steel rails in every main thoroughfare throughout the city and out into the distant suburbs of Killermont, Airdrie and Rouken Glen. The tram rail accommodated every twist and turn in the city centre street pattern, and even though this created some tight corners for the cars, such as the notorious turn from Sauchiehall Street into Renfield Street, they settled into their prescribed paths and Glaswegians crossed their city easily and cheaply. Electrification of the system followed in 1898 but the horses weren't finally retired until 1902. They would have been relieved. Pulling a packed tram up West Nile Street wouldn't have been much fun in a snowstorm.

Dalrymple was undisputed czar of the cars. A king of the road within the city boundaries, he ruled his rail-bound kingdom with a fountain pen sceptre, building up his fleet of Glasgow tramcars and the dedicated army of drivers and conductors it needed into a marvel of organisation and logistics. Tram frontiers stretched east to west from Uddingston to Dalmuir and north to south, from Bishopbriggs to Barrhead, all for fares that ranged from a half-penny going up a ha'penny a time to the top price of sixpence. This would take a whole family right across Glasgow, and bring them back home again for less than the price of a pint of beer.

Rattling along on rails that covered the city like an immense steel matrix, the 'caur' was everything to the Glaswegian. It was the pram carrying the new baby to see its gran, the tumbrel carrying the schoolboys to his exam, the shopping basket for the auld wifie in her shawls, the carriage taking the city Cinderella to the dance, a removal van for the newly-weds, a chariot for the football warrior, and an ambulance for the Saturday night drunk. Guided by gauntleted drivers, grim as granite, helped by conductors who were part-time Corporation employees and full-time comedians, supervised by austere, moustached inspectors dressed in superior green, the caurs were the practical mainstay of Glasgow's workaday routine. They were noisy and they shuddered and swayed but they were just right for Glasgow. They brought a bit of colour to our lives as well as to the patchwork of streets that they served. You knew where you were with a tramcar, because they never went off the rails. Why did they ever take them off the road?

ERL Fitzpayne was the next tram boss after Dalrymple. I learned his distinctive name early for it was written on the side of every tramcar and you couldn't help seeing it as you waited at the stop for your particular car to turn up. Ours was always a Number 9 if we were going into town by London Road, a 15 if we were going by the Gallowgate and if we were going in by Duke Street it was a Number 30. Each number was also a different colour just in case you weren't numerate. And if you were colour-blind you just asked somebody, 'Dis this caur go by...?'

Fitzpayne organised the debut of the smart, dome-shaped Coronation cars of 1937. These were the last word in modernity although George Bennie's ultra-modern railplane from seven years earlier still hung over the LNER railway line at Milngavie. The new cars included an honesty box where you inserted the fare if the conductor had missed you. ('Aye, that'll be right.') But many did pay, which says something for Glasgow. When the women conductors came in with the Second World War they made sure they never missed you. It was difficult to get the better of a Glasgow clippie, remembered yet for her famous cry while trying to clear the platform of hangers-on: 'Come oan, get aff!'

The male conductor of the caur was also a character, and, as has been mentioned, a natural comic. One conductor on our route noticed that a man had got on one night with his slippers on. When he made to pay his fare, the conductor, noticing the slippers, asked him: 'Will ye be wantin' breakfast in yer seat, then?' This kind of quip went with the uniform, which is why the tram conductor made such a good part to play on the stage. In *Tapsalteerio*, the Citizens' Theatre Christmas pantomime of 1953, I was cast as the Demon King, but in one sketch I was disguised as 'Wullie Fitz-pain-in-the-neck'. I played him as a university student working his vacation on the cars and for the sketch I wore my own university scarf over the well-known green uniform, which I borrowed from my Uncle Hugh McNamee, who was a real tram conductor. My theme song in the show, written by the late Effie Morrison, was a parody on *The Irish Washerwoman*. The audiences seemed to enjoy it and hearing the 'ting-a-ling' of the real ticket machine, which I had slung round my neck. The patter-song was a bit of a diction test, as you will see from this excerpt:

> *Students on summer vacation from Varsity*
> *Frequently find a spondulical sparsity*
> *They can hardly frequent the many old bars that they*
> *Used to frequent with the cheque for their fees.*
> *Go on the cars and the dibs are immediate.*
> *Why waste your time with the body Collegiate,*
> *I'm doing fine, kidding on I'm an eejit,*
> *So sigh no more, laddies, and Gil-no-more-hill.*
>
> *Clippety-clip, ting-a-ling, ting-a-ling!*
> *Gie them the bell, tae pot wi' the passengers,*
> *Pick up and drop 'em beyond their stops*
> *From Dalmarnock tae Blairdardie.*

Trolleys and trams and the motor buses
And subways and trains are run by us as
A finishing school for swearing and cusses
For rich and for poor, 'until death do us part'.
Many's the 'damn', the 'dash' and the 'blast' you
Can hear as the tram goes clattering past you,
It's empty on top but it's going so fast you
Would need to be off to a twenty yard start.

<u>*Clippety-clip, etc – add last line:*</u>
'From Dalmuir tae Auchenshuggle'

Waiting in lines for Number Elevens,
But all you can see are sixes and sevens,
But wait for a couple of hours, and by heavens,
The number Elevens will come in a queue.
Subways are quicker, a two-minute service
But never go under the Clyde if you're nervous
The driver's a learner and folk canna bear his
Asking us if we're enjoying the view.

<u>*Clippety-clip, etc – add last line:*</u>
'From Belgrove tae Cowcaddens'

(Spoken)
Come oan, get aff – move right along the tram.
Room on the top for two – naw, no' you.
Here comes the Inspector – Damn!
[Exits, sounding bell]
Ting-a-ling, ting-a-ling...

The tramcar suited the Glasgow character. It was hard to be shy when you were cheek by jowl with your fellow-passengers or staring into their faces across a narrow walkway. You had to be friends in a tram. You all swayed together as it turned a sharp corner, and, on longer stretches, you often got a read of the newspaper beside you. This was public transport in every sense of the word. It was often a bit of a crush but room could always be found. I remember one big woman getting on a green Number 9 somewhere along London Road. By the size of her big message bag, she looked as if she might have been a trader at the Barras. Anyway, she stood there, filling the doorway from the platform, blocking out the conductor standing behind her. 'Is there room fur a wee wan?' she asked genially in a mannish voice. Everybody laughed but two men got up at once from the side and gave her the double seat she needed.

I still have one of the rare tram tickets issued to commemorate the last run of the cars in September 1962. I found it in my mother's address book when she died, along with a winning bingo card (she won fifty pounds one night). The tram ticket had been punched at Bridgeton Cross on a Number 9 that ran from Auchenshuggle to Anderston Cross. Just to see the names of the stages is to re-awaken a longing for a past order: Maukinfauld Road, Fraser Street, Kent Street. These were stages in the journey of life as well as signposts along the middle-of-the road route I was travelling, but I never realised that then. I only ever wanted to get to the next stop.

Cycling was a big craze in Glasgow between the wars. There were bikes like the McGregor, the Clyde and the Howe available and they were all made in Glasgow. The two Cairney boys, however, went upmarket with a Raleigh. It had a bright red frame and we kept it under the kitchen bed. We had to share the bike because there wasn't room under the bed to store two. Before they made tanks and shells, Beardmore's built motorbikes and one man in our street had a sidecar to go with his. He used to waken us up every Sunday morning, starting it up early to get away into the country somewhere. I can still see his wife huddled in the tiny sidecar, muffled up like an Eskimo, although they never went any further than Loch Lomond.

Cars were few after the war but there were models like the Riley, the Austin and the Morris on the streets and the Argyle could still be seen. The Argyle was the only motor made in Glasgow. The only one I ever saw was years later in a saleroom window in Finnieston, sometime during the sixties. It was a beautiful little green convertible, and I think it was an original.

The coming of the motor car changed Glasgow forever. Just as television sent everyone scurrying indoors from the street, and the wine stores drained the pubs of drinkers, so the car imposed its needs on the city and destroyed much of it in the process. It all seemed to happen so quickly. Roads sprang up where lanes had once been. Whole streets were obliterated to make way for motorways and the city-dwellers had to make do as best they could under new overpasses and over new underpasses. They also had to learn to survive beside sliproads and alongside roundabouts as the planners tried to keep pace with the tsunami of vehicles of all shapes and sizes that descended on the city centre daily.

Districts like Townhead and Anderston were ravished and Charing Cross, once so lovely with its Grand Hotel facing the curve of the splendid John Burnet tenement, was the victim of major planning blunders and has been permanently changed for the worse. Where the tramcar had accommodated the existing streets, these same streets were now truncated, extended or simply removed to suit the car. Historic and much-loved landmarks were bulldozed for the sake of vehicle access. The gregarious tram passenger had retreated behind his private windscreen to become part of the anonymous, faceless road machine. Yet these were the same Glasgow citizens who had once packed the trams and now jammed the roads but the new drivers changed with all the changes around them. They seemed to lose the basic Glasgow qualities of humour and acceptance once they got behind a steering wheel. The old tram banter gave way to road rage. The smell of petrol appeared to act as an unhealthy stimulant. Internal combustion became external. Everyone was suddenly in a hurry, and the slightest delay was life threatening. It was free-range chaos by courtesy of the traffic light and it could be very tiring. It's no accident that the most prominent part of the car in towns is the exhaust pipe.

Nowadays, you can't see Glasgow for cars. It used to be that one or two people in every street owned a car or had access to one. Now, statistically, one in two people own a car, and the other one gets one with the job. Kerbside cars are a permanent feature of most inner city streets. It is bumper to bumper street decoration at peak hours. Residential parking is a gift from the municipal gods and residents are only too happy to pay through the nose for the privilege. Next to the Holy Grail, finding a parking space in the inner city must be the most engrossing quest available to modern man. Urban parking is a nightmare all over the world and it is just as true for Glasgow. It is so bad in some parts that, to be sure of a space in the morning, you have to start looking the night before.

The truth is that there are too many cars in Glasgow. There are too many cars in the world. We have come a long way from the black Ford Tin Lizzie and the old car that used to be part of the family for years. Now it has to be upgraded at least every two years. The Argyle, Glasgow's own car, is now an antique in the Kelvingrove Art Gallery but I am certain it could do a job for someone today. But no, that wouldn't do, new wheels have to keep rolling off the assembly lines. Everybody is told that they must have a new car. Relentless advertising tells us that we need the latest, minimally-changed, state-of-the-art freedom-machine; the mobile sitting-room with all mod cons; part war-chariot, part visiting-card. The personalised number plate is only the latest phase in the ego statement that every car is. This is as true for Glasgow as it is for Moscow.

We identify with our cars. We *are* our cars. We make ourselves in their steel and chromium image, which is why we polish them till they gleam and we resent the slightest scratch or dent. These are personal and deeply felt wounds and an affront to our perceived status. Love me – love my car. Even the windows are darkened so that the driver remains even more securely imprisoned in his four-wheeled cave. Who is he hiding from? Himself perhaps? The truth is, horsepower is manpower – and womanpower. And if he drives his car as a weapon, hers is more of a beauty parlour, an infinitely preferable use.

Given car driving conditions today, and the social menace that it is, one can only regret that someone in Glasgow's Town Planning Department fifty years ago did not have the prescience to put Puck's girdle round the city centre from Cowcaddens down to the river and from Glasgow Cross to Charing Cross, and lay down walkways and pedestrian precincts and, above all, restore the tram. We might then have had a utopian city today, but it was not to be. Where's yer Jimmy Dalrymple noo?

The city fathers were hardly to blame. No one could have foreseen the positive blight the motor vehicle was to become and it is difficult to see what they can do about it now unless they ban the car altogether, and bring back the original horse power. What a wonderful sight that would be: a posse of bowler hats, briefcases strapped to the saddle, thundering down Sauchiehall Street and wheeling right at Renfield Street to get to their stabling down by the docks. Think of the upsurge in horse manure – a source for butane or the future biogas. Not to mention the saving it could be in ever-more expensive oil and petrol and all those countless man hours lost on the motorway.

Let's face it, modern freeway is anything but. Once on its concrete path you are channelled into lanes, instructed from gantries above, honked at from cars behind and obscured by gargantuan trucks in front. Even the scenery is limited to hoardings or the backside of shopping malls or cinema complexes. Then when you *do* spot the correct exit junction in time, you find yourself inching from traffic light to traffic light and taking daring decisions at roundabouts that raise your blood pressure as high as your petrol tank is low. If you could, you would gladly get out and walk across the top of the cars like Crocodile Dundee, anything to make a bit of progress.

Yet all this was done in the name of progress and Glasgow, just like every other big city, was swept along in the mad race to keep up with the unstoppable. We all know that Nature abhors a vacuum, well, so does the average motorist. As soon as an empty space appears in any street, it is claimed by a car. Our streets now have a metallic sheen rather the neutral opaque of asphalt and tarmacadam. Instead of using roadsweepers we should employ metal polishers.

Alas, despite everything, we have to accept the car as a fact of modern life as once the tram was in its generation. We have to live with car; its cost, its noise, its idiotic snob value, its rust and deterioration, and, most of all, for the poison it emits. It's as much a killer as the ancient fire-breathing dragon. A modern St George would have to wear a mask before he came near a car. Yes, we have to live with the thing. Or die from it.

It's amazing to think that the present megalopolis – with its motorways and high-rise monotonies, clogged streets endangering the city's arteries, the commercial bustle of the central business area – all grew out of that huddle of old stones by the side of a burn, where the ford (not the car) was its sole reason for being. If everything has its end in its beginning, then we must wait until Glasgow dwindles down again to that spine between the Townhead interchange and the Saltmarket where it touches the Clyde and the Molendinar breaks out from under Duke Street. Somehow, I feel that won't happen tomorrow.

Yet who knows what further transports of delight still await good old Glasgow? Perhaps they will deepen the Clyde once more and bring the big ships up to York Quay again. After all, the trading port was the root of the city's cosmopolitism and it gave the riverside its exoticism and vibrancy. How wonderful it would be to see funnels up-river again. After all, Clydeside has to do with ships and it would be quite natural to have them around us once more, and within easy walking distance from the posh hotels that now abound by the waterside.

Barges, too, might have another life yet. They may be less beautiful, but they too could transport Glasgow to a renewal of old pleasures. Not so long ago, people stepped on to a barge at Fife's Rosyth and stepped off in the centre of Glasgow. This was thanks to the Forth and Clyde Canal, once a viable and practical commercial thoroughfare. It was a colourful band of water drawn neatly across the waist of Scotland and it easily could be so again. The Monklands Canal is still in place and Port Dundas is ready and waiting. What could be more pleasant than to skim through the canal shallows to the sound of an outboard motor instead of having to endure the white-knuckled grasp of a steering wheel among a cavalcade of cars locked on the motorway only a barge-pole's length away?

A canal offers locks of another kind, happy punctuation in the easy glide from Forth to Clyde. The restoration of the canal is something that should happen – and soon. The waterway lends itself naturally to scenic upgrading and embellishment and would offer a very picturesque and practical amenity at the same time. Port Dundas could come into its own as Glasgow's 'Wee Venice'. After all, it's only minutes away from the Glasgow Concert Hall and Scottish Opera at the Theatre Royal. If the Doge's Palace can be re-built on Glasgow Green why can't the Theatre Royal become the Fenice Opera House of the future Glasgow?

> *Like the baseless fabric of this vision,*
> *The cloud-capp'd towers, the gorgeous palaces,*
> *The solemn temples, the great globe itself,*
> *Yea, all which it inherit, shall dissolve,*
> *And like this insubstantial pageant faded,*
> *Leave not a rack behind. We are such stuff*
> *As dreams are made on; and our little life*
> *Is rounded by a sleep.*

Shakespeare's Prospero, for all his magic powers, could never have foreseen the cloud-capp'd towers of Easterhouse, the gorgeous palaces of

46

Great Western Road or the solemn temples of 'Greek' Thomson, but he would have appreciated the very substantial pageant that the Mackintosh buildings make around the city today – but this is such stuff dreams are made on.

I had a dream too. It was that I took out that little, green Argyle sports car from the salesroom window at the corner of Corunna Street in Finnieston and drove her through the deserted streets in the early hours of the morning, which are the middle hours of the night. There was little or no traffic and the night air was sweet. I breathed it all in as the car purred its way through a magic townscape. Bustling Glasgow is a city of the day, full of business, which is only a busyness. My favourite Glasgow is a city of the night. Night flatters any city, especially in the rain, when wet reflections gleam in the streetlights, and the pavements look as if they are the shadowy banks of a river and there is nobody to be seen in the streets but cats. Though a good friend of mine said he once saw a fox trotting across Sauchiehall Street in the early hours of the morning. I don't know what he'd been drinking – my friend I mean.

Glasgow gives to the night like a courtesan. She rises and puts on her jewellery, especially designed for the occasion. High street lamps shine like yellow earrings, a necklet of neon is draped on dark buildings and across the horizon a rope of pearls is thrown carelessly over the housetops as if they, too, know they have to look good in the festival of light that is nocturnal Glasgow. This is when the city competes with the very stars themselves. Her night caress softens the eye and we see only what we want to see – the wide, blue-starred panorama that is my city asleep.

In my dream I sweep through the hushed streets before returning west to put my dream car back in its car-dealer's window. I walk round to the flat Alannah and I once had in St Vincent Crescent and from its high, Georgian windows I look out at the Finnieston crane and the night lights around and beyond it. I am in wonder at the sight of my native city in black velvet stretched out as far the eye can see. I look at her lying there below me, silent and still, and I adore her.

CHAPTER THREE

All the Glasgows

IF YOUR FACE FITS

THE TROUBLE WITH GLASGOW is that there are so many Glasgows, and each of them is certain that they are the only real one. Each district is its own village and those who live there find it hard to accept that there is life in the outer space that is the rest of the city. Each is convinced that his patch is the epicentre of that spinning world that is Planet Glasgow. Yet the truth is that, however big the place may seem to the casual eye, Glasgow is not what she was. She is shrinking. She is now the third provincial city in Britain after Birmingham and Manchester, but try and tell a Glaswegian that. To the man in the street, his city is still the greatest, the best, the most. And even though he has to admit that it is also the loudest, most brash and the even the untidiest metropolis in the country, it is a likeable loudness, an endearing brashness and it can always be tidied up.

Glasgow comes at you from all directions. North to south from Milngavie to Newton Mearns, and east to west from Hogganfield Loch almost to the banks of Loch Lomond is a large sweep either way and there is such scope within these limits that the very air is charged. If they could, they would make you pay for it. There is energy in the place, an almost palpable urban dynamism, which, if totally harnessed, could light up several cities. This is due to the fact that, of its near 600,000 citizens at the last count in 2003, it's the thirty-something age group that makes up by far the largest sector of its work force.

It is significant that these energisers, at the peak of their years and on the high slopes to career fulfillment, should be most evident in modern Glasgow. It is also telling that the city has the fewest old-age pensioners than any other city in Scotland. Some blame it on the wartime rationing or the fact that they never had oranges when young. Or it could be that they just made their money and decided to spend it on a castle in Spain rather than in Castlemilk. Whatever the reason, Glasgow is in the hands of the new achievers and this can only augur well.

If Parkhead is Glasgow's Balham, and Hillhead its Hampstead, then Milngavie is its Hemel Hempstead, holding itself somewhat apart and aloof from the *hoi polloi* to the south and west and very properly keeping its tartan skirt length modest despite a nodding acquaintance in the past with Rob Roy MacGregor. Milngavie sits at the start of the West Highland Way, and from its perch on Glasgow's rooftop keeps one eye on the mountain heights behind her and the other on the heights of fashion that surround her. Milngavie is not poor but she doesn't talk about it. She is not at all garrulous, like some of her Glasgow neighbours. She 'knows fine' but says little, because her lips are pursed most of the time, but she belies any primness by enjoying the occasional wild weekend with the bikers and hikers that abound in the wayside hostelries that are a feature of the area.

Milngavie is still a real village. It has funny wee shops that sell guns, and knives and fishhooks. People still come out from the city to walk around the reservoir, that ordered inland sea, which the one-time Glasgow Corporation made out of the water piped from Loch Katrine. Here, captured forever by a magnificent feat of Victorian engineering, is the sparkling drinking water that was brought to the swan-necked wells rising from iron sinks in tenements all over Glasgow, and, incidentally, created an ongoing countryside leisure amenity.

To buy a house in Milngavie was always a good move. The trouble is that few Glaswegians, especially now, can afford to, so the place attracts foreign finance from all parts, and incomers have arrived from as far away as Edinburgh. A much-loved son-in-law of mine is an example. Derek is from Liberton in Edinburgh, but Milngavie has claimed him, as it has so many other artists, writers and musicians. They live in the splendid mansions, sturdy villas and neat little bungalows, which reach out manicured tentacles in all directions. Every lawn here looks as if it had been cut by scissors. It's hard to remember that this fastidious quarter is the gateway to the Highlands, to the land of the mountain and the flood. Yet, on some mornings in Milngavie, when the white mist hangs head-high, you are sure you can smell the peat-fire smoke and hear the pibroch on the hill.

How fitting that a blue tramcar served Milngavie in former days. Blue is just the right colour, vivid yet austere. The blue tram, incidentally, went all the way south to Shawlands, which, in its way, is a mirror image of Milngavie, except it reflects more the English home counties than the Scottish Highlands. Shawlands is very much of the Glasgow South; sedate and secure, but still pining for its former rural, wooded state.

Shawlands would have made a lovely little country town on its own had Glasgow not bullied it into joining the municipal firm. It still has traces of the bucolic. People remember a time when fields came all the way up to Crossmyloof station and Shawlands had its own ice-rink. The ice-rink has gone now but there are still standards to be maintained. There was a time in Shawlands when the professional at the Clydesdale Cricket Club had to enter the pavilion from a different door to that used by the amateur 'gentleman'.

They had real gentry here, however, in the Maxwells, who owned the Pollok Estate before it became the site of the Burrell Collection. You feel that Shawlands should still be dressed in good, country tweeds and not be pressed into a city suit. However, it was easy to get to other places from Shawlands Cross. You could cycle from here to Loch Lomond or go the other way and walk to Hampden. Getting to Scotland's national stadium allows a glimpse of the other Glasgows along the way. Clarkston comes first but you can hardly see it for houses. It is nothing but houses, back to back and facing, up hill and down dale, relentlessly pursuing the mortgage although many look as if they've been paid up long ago. Places like this are real dormitory districts because they look as if everyone's asleep in their flowerbeds. Newlands, on the other hand, is up and about, its well-kept villas exuding an air of unruffled professionalism. Giffnock is where the well-heeled pensioner has come to roost in smart, made-to-measure homes. There are no tenements here. Stairs are few and steps low. It is as if it had all been made for easy wheelchair access. Which is why, no doubt, it's a popular retreat zone for retired football players.

Whitecraigs boasts one of the most select golf clubs in Glasgow and is quite in keeping with a place where people have first names like 'Cameron' and 'Lindsay' and 'Grant', which are all surnames to the rest of us. What's in a name? Quite a lot actually and usually the better kind of name goes with the better kind of district. People who live in places like Whitecraigs wear collars and ties even on Saturdays, and during the week, those who still work do so in banks and offices. There are few pale faces to be seen. This is pink skin territory – evidence of good diet and regular holidays. No fish-n-chips here. It's more a question of fission microchips. There are brains to borrow behind the fitted curtains. In addition, the pillars of the establishment are firmly rooted and not even a Glasgow Samson from Newton Mearns would dare pull them down.

Samson, of course, was a good Jewish boy who would have been quite at home in Newton Mearns. Like Samson, it's a place that well knows its own strengths and plays to them. It realises that it is not quite Whitecraigs, but it keeps up a show, and who needs a golf course? With its strong Israelite component, the language here is more often Hebrew, for this leafy overspill from the Gorbals is Glasgow's Jerusalem. Money still talks louder here but not in a vulgar voice. The tone is soft but the meaning is clear: if you want it, you have to pay for it.

The houses are mansions and the last word in plush. Walk up the pink gravel drive and you feel dwarfed by the pine trees and the firs in the garden. The heavy front door opens on to another world, one with the hint of the exotic about it. There is obviously money here but there is taste to go with it, and all the evidence of travel and exposure to the best. There are no tenement restrictions here. Somehow I feel there isn't a red Raleigh racing bike under the bed. There is more likely to be an old, rolled up Aubusson carpet or a spare Vermeer.

Going east from here is hardly likely to bring you to Samarkand. Instead, it will take you through the Gorbals and over the Clyde by the St Andrew's Suspension Bridge and through the Green to Bridgeton Cross and the start of the East End. The colour here is green, for all green cars go east in Glasgow, but it might just as easily be red because the Independent Labour Party had its roots here with Jimmy Maxton *et al.* He and people like John Wheatley in Shettleston, and later Sir Patrick

Dolan and John McGovern MP, gave ordinary workers at least a nominal voice in the land.

The local accent might still bear traces of the large Irish influx, but Bridgeton, Parkhead, Shettleston and Tollcross remain the work places of the city, however vitiated. If, today, the steelworks, the forges, the foundries and the factories are all gone, you can still hear the clang of the steam-hammer in the street tones, see the factory smoke that is still in the eyes of the smaller, more pinched Glaswegians who populate the security-obsessed, refurbished tenements.

They can clean the stone work all they like but it's hard to get rid of the grit that sticks in the mind of the lower, working-class citizens. It is something that is deeply embedded in the subconscious and gives to a certain type of Glaswegian the kind of deep-throat voice that makes you want to clear your own. Yet he remains defiant. Why not? You can risk everything you've got when you've nothing to lose.

The plain streets here have plain names, although Salamanca Street stands out, but who knows much about the Peninsular War these days? Admittedly, Duke Street might owe something to the Duke of Wellington. This would be no more than appropriate. Since the Duke was tall and thin, he has given his name to the longest street in Glasgow. It begins at Parkhead Cross, and leads all the way west to the High Street, the site of the old university and the source of Glasgow's Molendinar beginnings. From here the city spread out to all points of the compass.

You can see this in the layout of its many parks. Glasgow was green before green was fashionable. Thanks to the foresight of our sooty Victorian forbears, there are plenty of parks in Glasgow. I am talking about open spaces, dear green places that bring the countryside right into the heart of the town. They have their own green glory and they come in every size from street-side patch to rolling acres, but every district has its masonry escape. No locality was spared its mandatory tree and bit of grass. What everyone in the city had in common was common ground. This was altruistic forward planning of a high order, for its benefits are still enjoyed today by the Glasgow ratepayer.

The public parks alone go a long way to atone for some of the architectural sins our City Fathers, in their ignorance, have committed, for the local park holds all of Glasgow in its green hand and its fingers spoke out in all directions. A park trek would be possible right round Glasgow. It would provide a very pleasing green safari for anyone prepared to walk the walk that is available from park to park. From Erskine to Bothwell, Kilsyth to Eaglesham and at all points in between, these verdant enclosures lie at the heart of every district.

Even if they do vary a lot in size and style they offer a very welcome sniff of chlorophyll on a dull, urban day. It is an easily accessible, off-street pick-me-up and, best of all, it is free. Almost any pastime or sporting pursuit is possible in the parks – and also some pursuits which are not so sporting, but give the parties concerned much amusement and pleasure. There is no need to beat about the bush here. The birds and the bees could have learned a lot on a fine night in the park. Any street map will get you to the park gates nearest you, and after that, it is whither where you wander. There is a remarkable range of choice, even today, but what is most appealing is that there is freedom itself. To make the park trek is to confer on yourself the real freedom of the city. Once among the greenery you can breathe deeply and let it all hang out. Litterlouts don't frequent parks in large numbers, as it's not so easy to write graffiti on a hedgerow.

All parks are good places, kind places. They open their gates and just let everyone walk all over them. They are the green signposts that point the way to all the villages that make up the conglomerate called Glasgow. Right at the centre is the Glasgow Green, one of the finest urban green spaces in Europe. This ancient open space on the northside riverbank stretching from the Saltmarket east to Shawfield is almost a district in itself. In its time, Glasgow Green has hosted armies, housed carnivals and harboured every kind of demonstration and parade. However, even with the terracotta Doulton Fountain in its confines, the Green is not a pretty place. It has few monuments, apart from the inevitable obelisk to Lord Nelson. There are nearly as many monuments to the hero of Trafalgar in Scotland as there are to Burns, but a vertical erection is an apt image for that 'one-armed adulterer', as he was called by some of Glasgow's gruffer inhabitants. The McLennan Arch at the Charlotte Street entrance is an Arc de Triomphe of municipal assertion but really it leads nowhere, except to that corner where hoarse, soapbox orators waste their substance on the Sunday air.

The whole place is a practical, grass environment created for the serious purpose of open air leisure with no frills attached. Rain cover is provided by the ever-popular People's Palace Museum, which stands at its very centre ready with a cup of tea, a touch of flora and fauna and the best collection of local artefacts ever assembled under one Glasgow roof. It's a jumble of bits and pieces, odds and ends and miscellaneous bric-a-brac which is not conventional museum matter but real, in-your-face stuff of the people. There is unblinking honesty in every nook and cranny. The building breathes the life and blood of its citizens. This is the real Glasgow on view.

Pride of the north is Springburn Park, a gift to Glasgow by the Reid family. It looks down on the rest of Glasgow from its seven hills, the highest point in the city. They used to say if you want to rise in the world you had to go to Springburn. The view from Sighthill Cemetery is still spectacular, although it's not one appreciated by its principal inhabitants. Springburn Park served as a holiday resort for the railway families of Springburn when even 'doon the watter' was expensive. The park had everything to serve the mind and body and even yet it is a valuable resource to the community. And its splendid North Glasgow College, born out of the old offices of the North British Locomotive Works, has to be seen to be believed. Springburn gave more to Glasgow than Molly Weir and her big brother, Tom. It gave the world its railways. So it's owed something back, surely?

The East End has its Tollcross Park opposite the magnificent tenements of Deer Park Gardens. Lying as it does like a wooded hinterland between gallus Shettleston and genteel Sandyhills, Tollcross Park is a veritable world in miniature. From the mansion houses at Enterkin Street you could keek through the park railings and imagine you were looking on to a Perthshire estate. Beyond its many gates there is a Highland Glen complete with gurgling burn and a wee stone brig. There is a formal layout of flower beds and symmetrical paths that would do justice to Versailles and the windswept football pitches high on the hill give views on to distant Springburn making it look, on good days, like Tuscany. Very distracting if you were a discerning footballer.

The old tennis courts and bowling greens were all out of the Edwardian age, and players did wear white shirts and trousers – even white sannies. Now there's posh. The Gatehouses were Victorian and straight out of any novel of that ornate age. You could easily imagine a pony-trap at the door. The world of the park was virtual reality with shrubbery. It wasn't black and white and realistic like the world beyond its railings. Against a green backdrop it displayed all the colours between sin and sanctity. It was horticulture as human culture, with a touch of local history.

Dennistoun was, and is, superior East End. My own mother's Parkhead dream was to have a house in Dennistoun with an inside bath. She got it eventually on Onslow Drive and never looked back. Some houses in Dennistoun are fit for a prince and still serve as fine homes for the working class aristocrats. Dennistoun's green spot is the stately Alexandra Park on Alexandra Parade. It is a smokier version of the West End Park at Kelvingrove. The trees are more black than green because of pollution from the nearby Blochairn Iron Works, but that just made them all the more striking. Today, the the iron works are gone but the trees remain, not quite so black-branched as they were, but they still have that East End look which says 'Take me as I am or don't take me at all'. They'll never lose that.

However, a superb vista is available to the lucky residents of Kennyhill Square, a genuinely superior tenement block that stretches all the way on up to Hogganfield Loch and the Letham Hill Golf Course beyond the Riddrie Knowes. Alexandra Park is decorous yet, borrowing something from the grace of King Edward's queen, who gave the place its name. Even the Number 6 tram used to make its sedate way along the Parade with all the dignity of a dowager. It didn't rattle along like the Number 9 did on our stretch of London Road on its way to Auchenshuggle. It was a very long tram journey, however, to the next park.

Rouken Glen was at the limit of parks to the south. It was another world altogether, but then no two parks are the same. They were set in different districts, and this difference showed in the kind of city park that resulted. It was as if they were in different climates. That's the charm of parks, they can be like whole other countries. Pollok Country Park, on the other hand, is more county than country. It doesn't have the ruggedness of Rouken Glen but it is entirely in keeping with the surrounding area – douce and unchallenging. The same might be said of Bellahouston Park, which was the site of the 1938 Empire Exhibition with its famous Tait's Tower, a short-lived Art Deco masterpiece worth at least a handful of Nelson monuments, but tragically lost to Glasgow because of war-time demands. It should be standing yet. Or ought it to be rebuilt like House for an Art Lover, which stands in the same park? They would complement each other beautifully but such a planning possibility would need another miracle of Mungo proportions.

The Clyde Tunnel comes out at Jordanhill and the beginning of Glasgow's West End. This is a whole other Glasgow. Proper but not prim, well spoken but not false, successful but not flash. A quiet good taste extends through most of its leafy thoroughfares. At its heart is Kelvingrove Park, surely Glasgow's prettiest green place with a statue to somebody every hundred yards to add to its interest, if not its attraction. The refurbished Kelvingrove Art Gallery stands in its grounds. If no great artwork in itself, it is a treasure house of the world's great art and gives a whole new meaning to Glasgow's propensity for 'going to the pictures'.

Looming over the gallery is the great stone mass that is the University on its Gilmorehill, looking for all the world like St Pancras Railway Station. This is no surprise as each was designed by the same man, Sir Gilbert Scott. On the other side of the park, beside the flagpole, steps lead up to the symmetrical beauty of Charles Wilson's Park Quadrant, showing off some of the finest domestic buildings in any European country. Here in the West End Park, West End chaps once sported their straw hats and striped blazers by the River Kelvin's many groves and strolled with girls who wore gloves and held umbrellas against the sun. Somehow, it still manages to retain its Edwardian atmosphere even in the rain. Even then it seems a whole world away from Parkhead. It's hard to believe these parks share a city.

Parkhead is now so synonymous with Celtic FC that it has swapped its old artisan vitality for the ingenuity of the pimp. It has become little more than one big parking space with hospitality and shelter for the Saturday hordes and the corporate sportsmen who play as enthusiasts for all the mid-week European Cup ties at the impressive Parkhead Stadium whose convivial demands are far beyond the half-time meat pie and cup of Bovril that served generations. Thousands of tenement homes have been demolished so that the new Celtic Stadium may stand revealed in all its incongruous giganticism. Even the graves of the adjacent Janefield Cemetery must have known the reverberation of the bulldozer as the football ground expanded over its walls to accommodate what has become Parkhead's latest service industry. The only radical element left in the district is in the layout and design of the massive Forge shopping centre.

We used to say of the Forge, 'Red sky at night, Beardmore's delight', because of the way the furnaces lit up the sky around what they called 'Parkhead Cathedral', but now that sparking glow has given way to neon lighting and somehow the sky's not the same. The din of the once mighty works has given way to the ping of the cash register. My father used to work at those Forge furnaces, as many of my pal's dads did, but it didn't take mine long to swap the stoker's shovel for the Union shop steward's pen just as wee Davie Kirkwood had done years before. Davie became a peer and moved to Bearsden. My dad would've made a good lord, too, but he'd never have moved to Bearsden. He would have preferred Mount Vernon.

If the East End isn't as red as it was, in every sense, there's a decided saffron shade to Glasgow's other areas in recent years, and in the more central districts the aroma of curry tends to engulf the old familiar reek of fish and chips. The cheaper wines have also displaced Barr's Irn Bru and there's no doubt that Glasgow looks upon itself as more cosmopolitan than metropolitan. Previously, cosmopolitan meant an acquaintance with continental films at a certain cinema on Rose Street, but now Glasgow is genuinely opening to the world, which may be no bad thing. It is extending a hand of friendship instead of offering the infamous Glasgow kiss (which might be described as an unexpected nod to the other person's nose). With such a negative image to live down, is diversity, both cultural and ethnic, not an unexpected advantage? Given the right mix, commonality might yet be possible.

2002 was designated as Glasgow's Year of Cultural Diversity and to acknowledge this, work was begun on a derelict site behind the old Tramway Shed on Albert Drive, Pollokshields, to create a new kind of landmark towards a deeper understanding between two different Glasgow peoples – the incursers and the indigenous – or the indignant, as they sometimes sound in the letter columns of *The Herald*. What was developed in Pollokshields was an imaginative concept called The Hidden Garden, which was aimed to provide a sanctuary, a garden of quiet, a contemplative space in a busy Glasgow area, in a manner that would be understood by every sect of every colour. Opened in 2003, it set the seal on yet another Glasgow response to the historical and cultural demands of contemporary society in a challenging and exciting way.

It is yet another green space, but one with a difference. It is regeneration for a cause. Pollokshields was chosen because it has the largest Asian population in Glasgow and the Sikhs have already built their Gurdwara there. The Hidden Garden celebrates the universality of nature and the human joy in being part of it. It is a respite and a refuge from the bigotry and conflict which were so much part of the city in quite recent times. The Hidden Garden is a sanctuary dedicated to peace.

Let's face it, for years the Salvation Army has been trying to do this in Glasgow and Methodist Churches were well known for what might be termed their outreach programmes for the needy of the parish, but their good works had the odour of charity rather than sanctity about them. This is not to belittle the good work these institutions did and still do, but The Hidden Garden appeals to instincts that are already embedded in the modern Glasgow.

There are 99 names for Allah in the Muslim religion and I am sure they are all uttered in this Pollokshields Garden from time to time for there are references here to everything that matters to the God-minded. The Five Pillars of Islam as well as the Five Sacred Trees of Buddhism are illustrated but there is no Celtic Cross in evidence, although Celtic music is served up on a Saturday with hot soup. Christmas carols are performed as part of the Diwali celebrations at the end of each year. Local plants vie with such exotica as magnolia, black bamboo and Chinese plum and one day, they say, there will be rammed earth bread oven. Somehow, you feel it will not produce a pan loaf.

The centrepiece in the garden is the stately Gingko tree, the oldest tree in the world, and at a time, every country in the globe had one. Now one can hardly believe that there's a tree growing in Pollokshields which is sacred to Asia and has protected the temples of the East for untold centuries. The fact that it now stands adjacent to the Tramway Shed was surely no accident, for this theatre has itself been the venue for so many innovative stage presentations in Glasgow.

Peter Brook's majestic production of *The Mahabharata*, the greatest story ever told in Indian literature and three times as long as the Bible, was a rare theatrical event that uncannily presaged the making of The Hidden Garden and it happened almost on the same spot more than a decade before. No one then could have foreseen that a building of such Asian significance could rise up in Pollokshields. Is this perhaps a sign of things to come? A Glasgow Apocalypse perhaps? As the seer, Nostradamus, might have put it:

> *The ground will rise up in George Square*
> *And pull all the statues down,*
> *Bells will ring out in derelict towers*

With great and ghostly sound,
A tree will spring up in Possil
And spread its branches wide.
And from Meadowside Quay to Ru'glen
Salmon will leap in the Clyde.
The river will silver along its length
Gleaming in burnished arc,
And a weegie will suddenly spread its wings
And fly over Tollcross Park.
A saffron veil over Pollok will lie
And peacocks strut on the Green
And the Glasgow Chinese
Will do as they please
In a City no longer Mean.

All this, I promise, will come to pass
Before years, one hundred and one go
It will surely get there
On a wing and a prayer
Or a miracle from St Mungo.

CHAPTER FOUR

Clyde Built

WHEN YOUR SHIP COMES IN

GLASGOW HAS BEEN sold down the river. Or perhaps, sold *on* the river would be more precise. As has been said already, it is a river city and just as it began with a handful of monks gathered at the ford, it has come back to the river as a focus for its latest development in the new millennium. It's more than a thousand years since Mungo made his watermark by the Clyde and the modern Clydeside waits to reap the benefit.

You could say that Glasgow was one of the many casualties of the First World War. The twenties did not roar for the keelies. Somehow their home town wasn't the same ebullient place it had been in Victorian and Edwardian times. It had already ceded its Second City of the Empire status to Birmingham. Who wanted such a title anyway, when there was no Empire left – not even on Sauchiehall Street? Glasgow didn't get a great press at the time, and it still doesn't, neither internationally nor even nationally. This is gradually changing though, and Glasgow will flourish again just as St Mungo said it would – and saints don't tell lies.

Especially Glasgow saints. He did say it would do so by the preaching of the word – well, the word is that Glasgow is on the rise again.

Glasgow is like the Old Testament – it has everything. Everything, that is, which is human and part of us all. It may have a violent edge but it is not an intrinsically violent place. Such an edge is only part of the drive that gives the city its particular spirit. Like a few million others, I have a fierce, partisan pride in this incredible place. In my eyes, it is by no means a mean city – anything but. I don't see it as grey and dirty and ugly as many are led to believe. I don't see it as pretty either. It's too honest for that. But look beyond the ludicrous shop fronts, the ridiculous high-rise apartment blocks, the miles and miles of recent housing drearydom and the inevitable writing on every wall, and you will see the real Glasgow.

It contains the finest surviving Victorian architecture in Britain, and at almost every corner of the city centre you will find evidence of its once great wealth and aesthetic attainment. But you have to look for these things. They're not easy to find because they're not immediately obvious. Glasgow is actually rather shy about its better points, so you have to lift your eyes, not unto the hills but to the sills of the second storey, for Glasgow is a city that was built from the first floor up. In a sense, it is still a second city; that is, a city best seen on the second floor, because, at that level, it is second to none. In fact, the best viewpoint might be gained from the top of a bus. Just glance out of the window and you may find a bearded, stone face glaring back at you, or the demure look of a maiden in mortar, or even the mouth of a fish.

Yes, lift your eyes from the pavements, above the parking meters, the traffic lights, all the clutter of modern street furniture; and you will see the Glasgow our great-grandparents knew and loved. Theirs was a stately and splendid metropolis, quality-built and made to last. Our top-hatted forefathers were convinced that progress would continue forever and as long as they were in charge, things could only get better. That was the Victorian way of looking at life. Their own mortality must have come as something of a shock to them. They would have suffered a greater shock however, to see how their burgeoning city had declined in the first half of the twentieth century.

During the twenties and thirties, it was as if Glasgow got sick and had to take to its bed. Starved of the heavy industries that had sustained it for a century, it lost a lot of weight in prestige and standing, and was in danger of turning its face to the nearest gable wall. It was a changed face, scarred by its many self-inflicted wounds, unable to call on its famous energy, because it was losing too much lifeblood as half its spiky population fled to kinder places. Glasgow was suffering tuberculosis of the soul. How ironic that in our own day, the face of Glasgow is changing yet again. But this time it's for the better: this time it's a bloodletting.

Instead of wasting away, it is now being laid waste, and from the fresh spaces found, the new Glasgow is rising on all sides, built on the solid foundation of the best of what went before. This basis is well nigh indestructible, so perhaps the Victorians weren't so wrong about their immortality. Glasgow is indeed a once and future city but at present it is in the throes of its own metamorphosis. Many who remember the old Glasgow are perplexed by its state today and have little affection for its sports centres and shopping malls and maze of motorways. They have no fond feeling at all for the layabout leprosy that spreads if it's not caught young. They deplore the rise of what is called the 'ned' culture, where the scum seems to have risen to the top. What must be realised, however, is that scum has no stamina and doesn't last long at the top. It soon drops back to where it belongs: at the bottom with the dregs.

All the little Glasgows huddle under the great dam of the big city. They cluster round its centre, each seeking its particular attention. It is this living dynamic which gives the place its excitement. All its differences make it a never-less-than-interesting whole. What is more, it is unashamedly eclectic. You can see a bit of everywhere just by walking the streets. Blythswood Square could well be in Edinburgh (except, perhaps, when the prostitutes patrol). There is a whole 'New Town' around Park Circus, and there are crescents in the same district that belong to the better parts of Dublin. There are Egyptian columns in houses along Nithsdale Road, and a Pugin Church in McAslin Street. See the Parthenon in Exchange Square and look for Paris along Great Western Road. See Naples and die, so they say, but see Glasgow and live. *See Glasgow...?*

We have our own Necropolis at Townhead, and the City of London can be glimpsed in frontages like the Glasgow Stock Exchange, the Athenaeum, and in at least half a dozen banks in the central business district. Bath's Beau Brummel would feel quite at home in Finnieston's St Vincent Crescent and Nash would still recognise Carlton Place. Is there a more lissome bridge outside Joyce's Dublin than the slender span hung over the Clyde at this point? Then, of course, there are the obvious landmarks: the University on its Gilmorehill which looks down on the superb Kelvingrove Art Gallery, which doesn't deserve being looked down on by anybody. Next to the Royal Infirmary at Townhead we have the ancient Cathedral of St Mungo. Strictly speaking, as the ecclesiastical purists know, it is not a cathedral. This may only be a terminological nicety but, like St Giles in Edinburgh, St Mungo's is an ex-cathedral, since it is no longer the seat of a bishop. It is surely no compliment to the beliefs of good Presbyterians to use the ancient title for their chief building when they don't approve of bishops. Or is it merely the case that, as with so many things tarnished by time, old habits die hard?

Glasgow has two actual cathedrals, the aforementioned Roman Catholic St Andrew's on Clyde Street and the Episcopalian St Mary's on Great Western Road. Religion generally hasn't gone unnoticed in the city. It boasts mosques and synagogues, temples and chapels and endless sober meeting places of every shade of piety from fundamental vermilion to genteel, social pink. There is accommodation here for all denominations and non-denominations. It can be seen then that St Mungo's influence has not been entirely lost even though it must be confessed that Glasgow's multivarious spires are more derelict than dreaming.

Glasgow's Victorian middle-class confidence is exemplified by the City Chambers in George Square; the People's Palace in Glasgow Green reflects the city's continuing proletarian base; and evidence of its medieval roots are in the Cathedral and across the High Street from it in the oldest building in the city, Provand's Lordship. It would seem that the entire art world to date is housed in the updated and renewed Kelvingrove Art Gallery, an international tone which is further enhanced by Alexander Thomson's Greek-style churches. And what could be more Glasgow impudent than the Templeton façade on Glasgow Green which can only be described as Venetian Ducal? There are sumptuous domestic dwellings in Kirklee and Pollokshields, and quaint little mews houses, quite William Morris some of them, within yards of the city's heaviest traffic.

But it must be said that when you think Glasgow you think tenement – that particular phenomenon which is undoubtedly the badge of Glasgow, old and new. There are glorious statements in stone by architects like Burnet, Salmon, Honeyman, Sellars and others, that command the eye at every Cross – Glasgow, Parkhead, Bridgeton, Anniesland, Partick and Charing. These are all crosses we bear happily for most of them show off the best of the tenements. These buildings stoutly resisted the wasting of time as much as they did the demolisher's ball in the sixties. Thanks to the efforts of the 1979 St Mungo Prizewinner, Mrs Dorothy Henderson, the better ones were cleaned and restored rather than being laboriously reduced to rubble.

There are more bingo halls than cinemas in Glasgow these days but we do have our own opera house, our own symphony orchestra, a ballet company, half a dozen thriving theatres and in the Mitchell Library in Anderston, we have one of the finest reading and research centres in Europe. However, there are also newer things to see, such as the Burrell Collection, a monument to the cupidity of one particular Glaswegian, the late Sir William Burrell, who spent his money on following his own taste in *objets d'art* from all over the world. Some of which, one suspects, were as much prised as prized. When Sir William found he couldn't take his possessions with him when he died, he donated the entire collection to his native city. This led to the creation of an adventurous setting for these treasures, thus making the Burrell Collection in Pollok Park as it exists today something of an artefact in its own right.

This is matched, even surpassed some might say, by House for an Art Lover in Bellahouston Park. It was in this same park, within range of the floodlights from Ibrox Stadium, that a man was jogging one morning and had a brainwave. And that was to build Charles Rennie Mackintosh's 'House for An Art Lover' on a level site within its gates. The house had only existed as a well-documented scheme on paper but the jogger, a civil engineer to the name of Graham Roxburgh, thought the building could be realised using today's materials and technology. He was convinced that Mackintosh wanted it to be more than a competition entry, so he set to work to make it happen.

An Englishman, Roxburgh had moved to Glasgow years before and when he bought Craigie Hall across the road from Bellahouston Park, a house which Mackintosh himself had worked on, he was converted to the Mackintosh mode. He could see the 'House' site from his office window, and it was this panorama which gave him his brave idea. A decade later, after much trial and error and selfless determination, House for an Art Lover now stands on that very site, completely covering

Graham's footprints. Latterly the project had proved too much for one man and he had to seek council and professional help to save the project, but it is still a triumphant testament to one man's vision and now exists as a very beautiful part of Glasgow's contemporary building fabric. It is also a very successful arts and culture centre in its own right and can quite rightly be said to be yet another jewel in the Mackintosh crown that now rests so firmly on Glasgow's head.

Glasgow was taken aback by the great phenomenon of the rapid rise in popularity of Charles Rennie Mackintosh, one of Scotland's greatest artist-architects, in the eighties. So much so, that it led to what *Herald* columnist Tom Shields called the 'Charles Logo Mackintosh School of Architecture'. Professor Andy McMillan of the Mackintosh School of Architecture regretted that most postmodern architectural design is a copy of a copy of Mackintosh, then more the fifty years dead. McMillan went on to quote the Roman Emperor Augustus who was said to have found Rome 'a city of brick' and he had turned it into a 'city of marble'. The good professor worried that Glasgow was doing the very opposite. The problem was that Glasgow was struggling to get out of its dirty dungarees and is still trying to get used to its new coat of many colours.

The value of Mackintosh's buildings within the city is only now being recognised as the world heritage they are, and, just in time, they are restoring the Art School, his masterpiece, to pristine condition at a cost of millions. For a few million more they could blast away the huddle of non-descript buildings hiding the front facade from the sun. While they're at it, why don't they build the Mackintosh Concert Hall in the way they have recreated his House for an Art Lover? And in Kelvingrove Park where he intended it to be?

This would be an act completely in keeping with modern thinking. Lisbon has built its Casa del Musica, Copenhagen has its glass-walled opera house, Beijing's equivalent is the height of *avant-garde* and La Fenice in Rome has been lovingly restored to its eighteenth-century magnificence. A vast Glasgow Concert Hall complex arose out of the old bus station on Buchanan Street. Would it had been Toshie's work. His Concert Hall design is almost a hundred years old now, but it is still uncannily of today and if it was good enough for Frank Lloyd Wright to steal for a church design in the United States it is surely good enough to become a new Mackintosh site in the Glasgow of tomorrow.

This, of course, may be only one writer's wishful thinking but the recipe has been proved already at Pollok and Bellahouston Parks and one must agree that a good aesthetic precedent has been established. The old can be made anew. It might take a miracle or two, but miracles are already happening. People are coming back to live in the city centre again and they are breathing new life into masonry that many thought had been choked to death under a century of soot. Glasgow is beginning to look good. At every corner, lovely things are happening. A much-admired translation was Princes Square shopping centre on the new Buchanan Street pedestrian precinct but, on the other hand, when the Briggait was remodelled as a shopping centre it did not last long. It still felt like the old Fishmarket by the river.

All the same, a municipal revolution is taking place right under the citizens' noses. Some are put out of joint by the speed of it all, but none reject such change. It can't be turned down, because Glasgow is on the way up. With the cleaning of the tenements, the wally close was rediscovered in all its Art Nouveau glory and now people even pay to look at an old tenement flat on Buccleuch Street which, by a freak of neglect, was preserved exactly as it had been in the twenties. Not everyone was up to the new terminology, though. An architect friend, John Coleman, told me of his visiting a very rich client at her home, where the walls were covered with seriously expensive paintings. When he told her of the new fashion for Art Nouveau, she remarked blandly over her champagne flute, 'Yes, I think I've seen some of his work.'

To take Glasgow, you have to take it whole and it's a whole lot better than you would think. To see it properly, you have only to look closely and lift the seven veils of prejudice, predisposition, misinformation, false tradition, open bias, outright snobbery and unabashed native arrogance. The restoration and conversion go side by side with deprivation and aberration. With the preservation, there is also consternation – but overall, there is a dedication to make Glasgow GO. The place jumps.

Within its limits, Glasgow has everything, but much of it is latent; it takes time to discover its wealth of detail. The Molendinar burn, which Mungo knew, now lies buried beneath the asphalt but it is still there – an underground stream, biding its time. The hidden Glasgow is the same – a city as deep and old as any, and as worthy of its present, surprising dignity. The gangs have all gone – the Billy Boys, the Sally Boys, the Baltic Fleet, the Norman Conks, the Redskins and the Cumbies. They're all pop groups now. Yes, the old Glasgow is going, but an even older one is still there – if you have eyes to see it. Glasgow is busy making herself beautiful like any girl getting ready for a dance. And like any Glasgow girl, she isn't afraid of showing what she's got – and even though she might seem shy about it at first, she can take you aback by her very audacity.

This was shown when Glasgow competed with other cities in Britain for the Garden Festival of 1988. That this ex-heavy industrial centre should think it could come up smelling of roses was improbable enough, but what was unimaginable was that they would do so with such speed and with such flair. Liverpool had been the first British Garden Festival site in 1984, and since these two dynamic cities had so much in common, Glasgow was confident it could do as well, if not better. City betterment was now the new enthusiasm and harnessing a resurgent energy, it quickly got its act together. Once again it all happened on the river.

Filling in Princes Dock, the authorities now had a hundred-acre site to play with. With the help of the Scottish Development Agency, no less than three million trees were imported and planted in several thousand tonnes of soil opposite the Finnieston crane, still standing to remind people of the shipbuilding Glasgow that once was. Its stern outline was almost a reprimand to the superficialities of the amusement park that grew up within sight of its mighty steel arm. The theme of the Garden Festival was leisure and the community and its various attractions certainly showed that – the railway rides, the steamer trip, the tram excursions and the roller coaster.

There was a special 'High Street' recreated to show all the diversion in Glasgow's great buildings, and one permanent feature which would survive the summer life of the festival was Bell's Bridge, a footbridge leading to yet another huge hotel to be reflected in the water. And yet to come behind the string of riverside hotels was the Sydney Opera house in the guise of the Scottish Exhibition Centre backing on to the railway line at Finnieston. A whole new leisure complex would later arise in acres where once was all manufactured dirt and density. The elegant line of St Vincent Crescent would be revealed in all its Jane Austen splendour, blinking in disbelief at the panorama now set out before it.

If, as Robert Louis Stevenson insists, everyone lives by selling something, then Glasgow, the most adventurous city in Scotland, had to start again by selling itself. It had to somehow put its new self on show. A start was made in 1983 with 'The Pride of the Clyde' celebrations. Although openly tourist-based, this was nonetheless an attempt to throw some light on a city determined to redefine itself. It also marked the bicentenary of the Glasgow Stock Exchange, making it the oldest such Chamber in the English-speaking world. It was also the 200th birthday of the *Glasgow Herald,* making it senior to the *Old Thunderer* in London. If one also adds that 1883 saw the building begin on the City Chambers in George Square, it can be seen that 1983 was a difficult year to bypass.

It is estimated that there are about ten million people worldwide with Glasgow or West of Scotland roots. After all, there are other Glasgows in the world – in Jamaica and in the American states of Kentucky, Missouri, Montana and Virginia. There is also a New Glasgow in Nova Scotia and now NASA has announced that a rock on Mars has been named for Scotland's Second City. So it might be said that the original Glasgow lies between a rock and half-dozen hard-to-find-on-the-map places. A bold attempt was made to bring at least part of that huge overseas diaspora home for the year of celebration. Sightseeing tours and site visits were speedily arranged, though most of the old places that exiles might have liked to see again had been bulldozed or blown up. But much remained to be cherished – and exploited. Such as that intriguing square mile in the oldest part of Glasgow: from the High Street to George Square, and from Townhead down to Glasgow Cross; an area which was to become known as the Merchant City.

My own company at the time, Shanter Productions, was instrumental in interesting the city council in a Tontine Festival to spotlight this ancient rectangle which belongs to the very beginnings of Glasgow as a trading centre. It grew to its greatest prosperity just as the eighteenth-century tobacco merchants were making their pile in the Trongate and surrounds. This particular area, going north to George Street, had already been the subject of study and analysis by Jim Rae, the then City Director of Planning, and his team. To emphasise this historical and cultural propensity, Shanter Productions suggested the Tontine Festival as an autumn celebration, centred on the Candleriggs and the restored City Hall.

Why Tontine? Lorenzo Tonti was an Italian who, while in France during 1689, devised an insurance scheme designed to reward the survivor of any investment group in which the individual member agreed to subscribe during the lifetime of another named member and, in return, receive a proportional part of the group's profits. It obviously paid to live long, because the last survivor inherited everything. A Tontine Society was formed in Glasgow in 1781 and soon prospered. The last named party on the initial subscription was Miss Cecilia Douglas who died in 1861 at the age of 90, worth £7,000. The city had also gained the Tontine Hotel and some excellent new buildings within the Merchant City square mile.

I had the notion of applying these principles to theatrical projects like drama, dance and opera but since most of these enterprises live from day to day rather than from decade to decade it was difficult to organise from an actuarial point of view. I handed it over to more experienced accounting hands but sadly the whole proposal died of inertia within a couple of years. It might be still worth trying one day, but not by this writer. He is not so confident of reaching Miss Cecilia Douglas' 90 years.

While the Tontine Festival was dying of dust in the council files, another festive occasion was suddenly projected. This was a huge, and quite unexpected, sunburst which rose over the city horizon. It was called the 1990 European City of Culture; an international event, which was the equivalent of the artistic Olympics. Glasgow should never have been in the running. How the torch came into her grip is yet more proof of a striking capacity to rise to the big occasion with alacrity and complete confidence when required. What is even more fantastic to Glaswegians is that we pipped Edinburgh, home of the great International Festival of Music and Drama, for the honour, and they still can't believe it. But we keep reminding them.

The main reason for the successful bid was the teaming of the Glasgow District Council with the Strathclyde Region and their combined ability to raise the £50m to pay for it all. It was a triumph of cheek, which is the city's trademark, and it paid off completely. As part of the programme they created an underground exhibition of the city's history beneath the Central Railway Station and completed the aboveground Royal Concert Hall around the old bus station. Then they turned the tramway depot at Possilpark into an imaginative and exciting theatre space. It was here that John McGrath, an Edinburgh exile from Liverpool, created the first of several spectacular theatrical productions with his 7:84 company, beginning with *Border Warfare* in 1989 and continuing with *John Brown's Body* in 1990.

It was a big year for big events and that didn't just mean Pavarotti's filling the new Exhibition Centre. Also in that *annus mirabillis*, Bill Bryden, a Greenock man, wrote and directed *The Ship*, a mammoth theatrical production which would have done credit to Max Reinhardt. In it we saw, or seemed to see, a huge ship actually launched within the four high walls of a Harland and Wolff engine shed in Govan. It was a miracle of theatrical design and *mise-en-scene*, and the modern Glasgow stage has seen nothing finer, nor anything more appropriate to its triumphant Year of Culture. What was even more fitting was that this staging paid tribute to Clydeside and Glasgow's glorious shipbuilding history.

A whole line of liners, ladies all, have sailed down the slipways that used to adorn the docks from Whiteinch to Yoker, and gave names to ships that all the world knows. The *Comet*, the *Cutty Sark*, the *Aquitania, Lusitania*, the *Howe* and the *Hood*, and the two Queens, *Mary* and *Elizabeth*, all set out to sea, shaking off their Glasgow ropes. Alas, this Glasgow army of artist-tradesmen, virtuosi with the rivet and acetylene burner, carpenters who could turn over a Sheraton chair in a morning, is virtually no more, gradually reduced to impotence by Japanese cost-cutting and copycat ingenuity, but not before Red Clydeside had created a roll-call of marine masterpieces. Glasgow is remembered all the better for them.

Yet another ship image from the dry dock of memory was given to me by playwright Bob Adams of Aberdour, who remembers rural Shawlands from the twenties and the long, summer days when he and his brother Ian took their toy boats to Queen's Park to sail them on the pond. While there, they would see old men wearing blazers and yachting caps, using long poles to control very elegant yachts, which seemed almost seaworthy as they made their smooth journey across the mini-ocean that was Queen's Park pond. Each mini-voyage was carefully planned according to wind and current, and the old land-captains would coax their old land-legs around the perimeter so as to arrive at the little landing quay just as their model ships sailed in.

Sometimes, however, these proud vessels were becalmed in the middle of the pond and out of reach of the long pole. It was then that the ancient pond mariner, just as calm himself, would make for the nearest bench, take out his pipe, light up,and puffing happily, would stare out 'to sea' and will his craft home. It's a happy picture of mature resignation, the wisdom of the aged, the knowledge that everything has been before and will come again. It is also a lovely image with which to leave my city of Glasgow on the make – an old man, his job done, waiting patiently for his ship to come in.

Even as this book goes to press, the first new bridge to cross the river in thirty years has been built at the end of Finnieston Street. This stylish span is called the Clyde Arc but because of its deliberately wayward line Glaswegians already call it the 'Squinty Bridge'.

CHAPTER FIVE

Local Heroes

WEE WILLIE WINKIE

'LET US GIVE praise to illustrious men...'

The history of anywhere is the history of its famous men, and so it is for Glasgow, although it's a matter of debate as to who the most famous Glaswegian has been. Today, Billy Connolly would certainly have to be considered. He is to Glasgow what Sir Sean Connery is to Edinburgh, and it's surely no bad thing for any country when a former shipyard welder and an ex-milkman are held to be two of its most famous sons. This is all the stranger for the fact that each of these estimable and world-kent Scots is a genetic product of the nineteenth-century Irish diaspora that gave Lowland Scotland its labour force and two football clubs, Edinburgh's Hibernian and Glasgow's Celtic. So far, Dublin has made no claim on either man.

It may also be unfair to cite any product of the media as being famous. Their fame is a result of strenuous efforts on their behalf by many whose job it is to make their client's name and face known to as many as possible before the said client retreats behind dark glasses to attain incognito, which, paradoxically, is the ultimate level of world fame as Miss Garbo once exemplified. In the present age of 'sell-ebrity' as it might be called, fame can be bought and sold to the public according to the depth of the advertising purse, but real fame takes time and legends a little longer. Names may be made in the short term by the public relations machine, but the public makes its own heroes, and does so after its own fashion, and in its own time. Posterity will not be hurried. After all, it has all the time in the world – and the hereafter.

There is a mythic element involved. Memories of deeds done on whatever the field – whether performances seen on stage or screen, or incidents witnessed in real life – the best of which are crystallised and passed down through the generations by word of mouth, person to person, so that by a general osmosis someone, dead or alive, is gradually realised as a hero-figure. They then become champions in the fullest sense and by virtue of the singular and unique quality shown are examples to be cherished. Sometimes, as in Chinese Whispers, the passing on of their story renders the party concerned as bigger, better and more beautiful than they actually were but this may be excused as a natural heightening of the fact to make it fit the myth. We are not overly concerned with reality here. These people live on in the memory because so many memories go into the creating of any hero image.

Anyone has a fair claim to fame if they have a statue erected in their honour, especially if it is done so by public subscription; but for the most part, once these memorials in masonry are up and standing, dereliction sets in almost at once. This applies to the memory of the subject as much as to their stone or bronze or cast-iron representation. Glasgow has more than its fair share of statues and monuments to once-famous names and some of these deserve their stony place in the city's roll call of the great, while others are questionable to say the least. It still beats me why the highest statue in George Square should be one of Sir Walter Scott, who was born, bred and educated in Edinburgh and lost his heart, and most of his fortune, to Abbotsford in the Borders. Still, a good part of *Rob Roy* is set in Glasgow and the *Waverley* novels did inspire the naming of several junior football teams in the city. Unfortunately, that didn't stop them from folding up and taking the name with them.

Anyway, what's in a name? And what is any kind of fame worth in the long run? We can't take it with us, but our deeds are things that live on, and the more memorable of these is what constitutes our posterity.

This is what the hero leaves behind in one form or another, for the rest of time or for a fortnight. Not all heroes are forever. At best, the most famous of any age dwindle to a footnote in an obscure reference book – and fortunate to even get that. There is nothing more irrelevant than yesterday's newspaper, or older-looking for that matter, and so it is with yesterday's famous. The Duke of Wellington was a big man in his time but he is now inured in Exchange Square, exposed to all the elements with only the occasional red and white traffic cone as cover. It looked all the better for being squint. They should have left it there permanently. It was a typical Glasgow comment on what, after all, is a dated and outmoded convention. It was another two fingers offered to the hypocrisy of the public reputation as seen in an expensive accumulation of bronze.

Putting up statues to dead men was a big Victorian thing. They were thanatopsistic, obsessed by anything to do with dying, and many shed more tears over the death of 'Little Nell', a fiction of Dickens imagination, than that of their next of kin. Funerals were to be celebrated with an enthusiasm that bordered on necrolatry. The more plumed the horses and more ornate the cortege the better. Professional mourners were hired with the horses and new clothes were bought to be admired at the graveside. Even the corpse was dressed to die, if not to kill. Many an ordinary un-famous person of that era died possibly unaware that more was being spent on burying them than was ever used to keep them alive. Similarly, every tenement housewife, up to my own day at least, scrimped and saved to give the wee insurance man a penny a week to make sure she had a good funeral. She would rather die than be shamed in front of her neighbours.

It says something for Glasgow that its most famous statue was erected not to flatter some personage from history, but someone who didn't even exist. Lobby Dosser wasn't a real person at all but a character created by Bud Neil (for many years the cartoonist on the Glasgow *Evening Times)* for a nightly comic strip during the sixties where the action took place up the Calton Creek. It was gleefully adopted by the citizens of Glasgow and it ran nightly without a break for six years. It was surreal enough to appeal to the local zany streak yet it was rooted in an environment familiar to everyone. The name itself was from the tenements, the lobby being that narrow strip of the flat connecting the kitchen to the room or two rooms depending on the class of tenement. A 'dosser' was the unexpected guest, up for a wedding or a funeral, who had to borrow a cushion and sleep, or doss, under his own coat in the lobby for the night. Any overspill had to go out on the landing with several coats over them.

So Lobby Dosser got his name, and won his place as a Glasgow hero, via the persona of an urban cowboy out of nowhere. Glasgow connects with cowboys. You only have to think back to the visit of Roy Rogers and his horse, Trigger, to the city in 1956 and remember the thousands that turned out to see both canter up the steps and into the Central Hotel. Bud Neil knew this kind of Glasgow and it showed, although he gave the Dosser's horse, El Fideldo, two legs less than Trigger. Well, why not? You only need one leg to stand on, so El Fideldo had a spare. This was cartoon land, which Glasgow itself can be to the uninitiated – a place of bold strokes, large effects and a laugh at the edge of it all. In Glasgow, you have to laugh or you'll go daft – and what's dafter than a two-legged horse with a couple of men on its back? Seated behind Dosser is the villain of the piece, Rank Bajin, who could not have been called anything else. All three are now recreated in bronze and occupy a plinth on a green space off Woodlands Road, opposite the Halt Bar.

It was the idea of *Herald* columnist Tom Shields who raised enough money from his readers to commission designers Tony Morrow and Nick Gillon to create this odd street decoration. It shows Lobby Dosser on El Fideldo with Rank Bajin riding postilion looking as if they are heading for a curry at Charing Cross (which is now more Indian Territory than the Calton).

The work is silly but it's just right for the city. It's mad; an unreal mix of folklore and fancy, which manages to say something while at the same time being funny. That's how the average Glaswegian looks on life: it's unreal and funny. Even the villain is amusing. In Glasgow you always have to deal with a villain of some sort. It starts with the teacher, goes on to foreman, then the factor, and ends up with the publican – and every one of them a rank bad yin at times.

Of course, not all are villains but they represent the constant baffle wall of authority that stands to balk the average Glasgow man at every turn. This is what makes him appear belligerent, or impatient to say the least. Especially when he has no right to feel aggrieved whatsoever. That's when he's at his most dangerous – and most obscenely eloquent. This is when he seizes his own freedom of Glasgow and doesn't care who knows it. As the famous song puts it, 'Glasgow belongs to me'. And so it does until he sobers up. Unfortunately, the bronze Lobby Dosser can't sing along. He has no voice. This is a shame because his laconic comment in print was a big part of his attraction. But then he is, after all, a work of comic fiction.

Fiction-into-fact is just as true of Barrie's Peter Pan on Embankment in London or Stevenson's Alan Breck in Corstorphine in Edinburgh. They both came out of their writers' heads to be ossified artistically in bronze. They now palpably *exist*. It is almost impossible to believe that they were never real people. In a way they are more real to most than all the politicians, generals, ministers and town councillors who have warranted a perishable mortality. What statues, I wonder, might be put up if the present-day ratepayers had their say? Would they all be Glasgow film stars, like Robert Carlyle, who has had the sense to invest a million pounds in a family home in Partick? John Hannah is also one of our best-known actors but does anyone still remember the other John Hannah, an RAF aircrew sergeant from Scotstoun, who won a VC during the war? Or the Glasgow firemen who put out a blaze on a warship berthed at the Broomielaw before it blew up its cargo of ammunition? Had they failed, the blast would have taken out the city centre. All these men were *real* heroes, and we don't even know their names.

War has now become so obscene and distorted that even its heroes are discredited. Fanaticism has blinded us to what courage really means, and the high level of cynicism towards anything militaristic prevents a true appraisal of any act in war. What is brave to one side is a heinous crime to the other, so the public turns to escapism and looks for its heroes in sport or on television. To the Glasgow man, a football player is the nearest thing to God, so why not worship him while he is in his sporting heaven? Henrik Larsson, when with Celtic, would have had a whole Parthenon built for him at one time. Jackie Stewart, the former world champion racing driver, is also a possibility as a Glasgow deity, although he might more properly belong to Dumbarton. Andy Stewart, however, the Scottish Soldier singer-actor of recent happy memory, was born in Glasgow. The trouble is that showbiz reputations are not long lasting and might already be waning before the bronze is even cast. There is no trade more volatile in its public relations than that of the performer in the public eye. Few who have 'got there' today are still there tomorrow.

No matter how skilled or appreciated they may be, many who court this kind of fame last only as long as their own generation and only a few are allowed to grow old gracefully in their profession. By 'old' I mean forty-something. It's a lucky actor who still finds work while drawing the old-age pension. Most football players are only remembered if they become television presenters, like Alan Hansen and Ally McCoist. Even that flimsy resort is hardly a permanent or pensionable position. Who then, if not these evanescent, contemporary famous people, will make it on to the heroic plinth in our day? In short, whose name is likely to last? Goodness knows. Quite honestly, do we have a Glaswegian in any field with an unchallenged world status?

In fact, we have. He was Campbeltown-born but now lives in Bearsden and is an accountant at Strathclyde University. His name is Willie McCallum and he is, by universal acclaim, the greatest piper in the world. Bagpipes, however, annoy those cellphone Scots who sell their country as a brand. As far as they are concerned, it's just a knot of old men kicking up a racket, but the 'racket' Willie McCallum kicks up in one of the great pibrochs, is the music of all time and has a cultural standing equal to that of a Bach fugue. Yet Piper McCallum goes unhonoured and unsung in his own land, while revered around the world. Still, it must be hard to practise properly in Bearsden.

There are many Glaswegians like Mr McCallum, who have considerable prestige among their peers yet remain little-known outside their own world. Jim Watt, the boxer, was once a world-beater and Kenny Dalglish, the footballer, was in the same class. Both were Glasgow men and each earned the ultimate citizen's accolade of being given the freedom of their native city, but that didn't prevent Kenny emigrating to England, as did Sir Alex Ferguson, from Govan, who is also a freeman. Tommy Docherty is another very successful Anglo-Scot, and the very spirit of individual freedom but somehow I can't see his ever receiving the freedom of his native city or having a statue of himself being put up at Shettleston Cross – unless it could talk.

The freedom of the City of Glasgow is the highest mark of respect the municipality can offer any person of distinction or quality, or one who, in the eyes of the Lord Provost and the City Council, has 'rendered eminent service to the City'. It is in effect a civic honour, and one not trivially bestowed. Of itself, it confers no rights or privileges on the recipients, but no one has been known to refuse. The Royal Family, naturally, is represented in every generation and each of their formal names and titles take up a page each, but the most exciting royal link with Glasgow was made when HRH Princess Margaret accepted the Freedom of Entry on behalf of the Highland Light Infantry, the city's own regiment, of which she was the Honorary Colonel-in-Chief. It must have been a stirring and echoing day in the marble halls of the City Chambers when the Colonel, Officers and Other Ranks entered behind their pipes and drums with bayonets fixed and colours flying. Had the Other Ranks had their way, they would have marched straight to the bar, and their Honorary Colonel would have been the last to object. Sadly, since that proud day, Princess Margaret has died and the HLI has been disbanded.

The gilded cavalcade of the great, the good and the godly that is the roster of those who have been given the Freedom of Entry to the City is evidence that Glasgow has kept her window to the world open; not only so it may see out but that the rest of the world might now and then look in. However, one of the missing international names on the Freeman list is Robert Service who is, in my opinion, the most successful writer ever produced by Glasgow. Although born in Preston, England, he was raised in Kilwinning, Ayrshire and educated at Hillhead High in Glasgow and then at Glasgow University before becoming a bank clerk like his father. At 21, he fled from a Glasgow bank to the Yukon where, to while away the time among the snows, he began to scribble verse. His books of easy rhyme sold out before they even reached the bookshops, being bought out by the printers themselves. He resigned from the bank to become a full-time writer and, eventually, a millionaire with a home in France and a name in Hollywood.

> *Though my stomach be concave, and my hair no longer*
> *wavy,*
> *Though I have one foot in the grave, the other's in the*
> *gravy.*

Service settled in France permanently, but, as has been said many times, you can take the man out of Glasgow... This can be seen in one of his typical verses, 'Bindle Stiff', when he gives a glimpse of the Glasgow he knew:

When I was a brash and gallant gay
Just fifty years ago,
I hit the ties and beat my way
From Maine to Mexico.
For though to Glasgow, gutter-bred,
A hobo heart had I,
And followed where adventure led
Beneath a brazen sky.
And as I tramped the railway track,
I owned a single shirt.
Like canny Scot, I bought it black
So's not to show the dirt!
A handkerchief held all my gear
As I set out to roam,
I was a feckless lad I fear
With all the world for home.
But I would think, each diamond dawn
Of how I forged my fate.
Where now the Gorbals and the Tron?
Where now the Gallowgate?

There are many other famous Glasgow names which have gone unhonoured, well known in their day but now missing, presumed forgotten. It seems fitting, nevertheless, that we should remember our artists. We wouldn't have room for all our comedians or singers but Glasgow-born poet, Thomas Campbell, has his place with Burns in George Square, so why isn't there a place for William Miller, the Tollcross rhymer, or better still, his creation, 'Wee Willie Winkie'? Like Lobby Dosser, Wee Willie Winkie is fictional but he is still very real to many Glasgow children, even today. He started off in Tollcross, when William Miller, a wood-turner whose hobby was writing children's songs, had them published first in 1863. Who born in Glasgow doesn't know the little refrain:

Wee Willie Winkie goes rinnin' thro' the toon,
Upstairs and doonstairs in his nicht-goon,
Keekin' at the windae, tirlin' at the lock,
Tellin' weans tae get tae bed,
It's past six o'clock...

If we must have statues in the city then away with beards and medals, top hats and horses and let's have a neat little statue of Wee Willie at Parkhead Cross, holding a clock under one arm and pointing along to Tollcross Park with the other. That would honour Mr Miller and delight the children. What Glasgow really needs is more artworks like the daft Dosser or St Mungo's Bird in the Buchanan Street precinct.

These things represent the adventures of the mind, but Glasgow also has its share of real adventurers and 'daft' might be exactly the word to describe some of the most recent examples. For example, the small army of carefree keelies who left Glasgow in the fifties on subsidised passages to places like Toronto where they were to found new Glasgows within that Canadian metropolis and make their mark as entrepreneurs and purveyors of all things Scottish. Some of them went out with not much more than the clothes they stood up in, which for many was a shiny demob suit, a tie with a big Windsor knot and winkle-picker shoes. A raincoat was a luxury, a hat a non-event and gloves were never even thought of. If they had a scarf at all, it would have been blue and white or green and white. Thus attired, they faced their first Canadian winter with its Polar temperatures and snowdrifts at the door that were often taller than they were.

Yet this bantam brigade somehow dug themselves out, and even if hands and faces were red and raw and noses froze, they dug for themselves a place in Canadian life and you can be sure by the next Toronto blizzard they had the fur hats, anoraks and gauntlets, not to mention the thermal underwear. If the winkle-pickers had lasted they were kept for the dances organised by local Greek or Italian social clubs. The Scots never seemed to have a club of their own. They couldn't even agree who was to be on the committee to help organise one. Where two or more Scots are gathered together, there you have continued room for debate.

What they were in accord about, however, was in making a fist of it in a new country. It's the people who make any place, and these people were out to make their presence felt. Glasgow grit was called on and successful businesses were set up. The immediate results were shown in the big houses many were able to buy in the Toronto suburbs. In these wood and stone two-car mansions, the pride of place was the below-ground recreation room which somehow, despite its plush leisure furnishings, managed to convey the atmosphere of the cosy-room-and-kitchen many of them had left less than a decade before. The place was heavy with Glasgow memorabilia: prints of tramcars and tenements, pictures of football teams, school photos, and wally dugs on the mantlepiece above the huge log fire. In one house they even had an old pulley hanging from the ceiling. It was lowered and used as a hammock on occasions.

You could always spot the Glaswegians in Toronto in the seventies. They had big cars and in the back seat were copies of the *Sunday Post* and *Sunday Mail* collected directly from the Prestwick plane at the airport and distributed 'among their ain' along with square sausages from the Scottish butcher, scones from the Scottish bakery and the latest Sydney Devine record from the Scottish music shop. The Jews could have learned from these Glasgow expatriates about inclusiveness, and what was considered *kosher* in Canada. What they shared with their Jewish pals was *chuzpah*, and they never lost this impish energy no matter how cold it became.

These men are now grandfathers and their dynasties are secure in their adopted country, just as others are in the United States, South Africa, Australia and to a lesser extent, in New Zealand. Their children and grandchildren are less tied by the umbilical cord to Glasgow, but they pay lip service to this heritage by packing out every Billy Connolly concert when it comes their way. In remembering their parents' roots, they are maintaining its part in their own future. They don't need to build statues any more; they have the Internet to encapsulate their heroes. Previous generations gave their memorials a permanent shape capable of surviving not only the weather, the tag artists and the desecrators, but also the scrutiny of a posterity who might not even know their names – but everybody knows Billy Connolly.

Billy creates Glasgow wherever he goes but it depresses me to think that its image is still regarded, especially in London, as *No Mean City*. This was the title of a very average book which caused a sensation when it first came out in 1935 at the height, or rather, in the depths, of the Depression. It was hacked out by a London journalist, H Kingsley Long, and an out-of-work Gorbals labourer, Alec MacArthur, and created the picture of Glasgow that many see even now. These people are the kind who make the detour to Edinburgh when driving from England just to avoid Glasgow.

To their credit, the co-writers tried to put their aspect in its true perspective by stating in their preface:

> The authors wish to state that their novel deals only with one seam in the crowded life of the Empire's Second City. In their view unemployment and overcrowding are primarily responsible for conditions which may be paralleled in all great cities, but which are, perhaps, more conspicuous in Glasgow than in any other...

This worthy disclaimer, however, is lessened by their appendix, which, while stressing that the book is fiction and the characters completely imaginary, cites press reports of court cases dealing with the activities of gangs and their girls in the slums of the East End and Southside. It was obvious that these misguided youths were playing out the Hollywood fantasies, which too often made a hero out of the hoodlum, but the result was that the reader put down the book as if they too had just been slashed across the face with a razor.

Glasgow, the same Glasgow that had hosted kings and queens, dukes and duchesses, peers and prelates, generals and admirals and all the famous names of the day at banquets in the City Chambers, now had to live with this vicious image of itself for the next fifty years. Fortunately, at the end of that time, better Glasgow writers had been born and published, the slums had been blown up, the remaining tenements cleaned and Glasgow became, once again, the warm sandstone place it had been before the soot and the smog got to it. Nowadays, visitors come to see this transformation for themselves and can hardly believe it – Glasgow is almost beautiful again. Almost, but not quite. Ugly uniformity is the rule in the business centre and where debris doesn't manage to ruin the urban landscape as seen from any inner-city hotel, the ubiquitous graffiti does. But then what metropolis in the world is any different? Paint spray rules – OK? Despite this, visitors have returned to the city in recent years like a long-forgotten migration. These days, it is no longer necessary for them to make the detour to Edinburgh.

So, stands Glasgow where she did? Not quite. There's no need for the worthy plinth today; she is a website now, and growing. We can therefore leave the old famous on their pedestals and welcome our new heroes as they rise. As Burns might have said, 'let time and chance determine wha will stand or fa'. The rest of us must be content, meanwhile, to keep our feet on the ground; down there in the dust from whence we came and where, without doubt, we will all surely return. Meantime, somewhere, something stirs and a memory lingers on...

Riding into the sunset of Calton Creek, goes our hero, Lobby Dosser, on his trusty El Fideldo with Rank Bajin, finally defeated, slumped across the saddle. And running up behind them comes Wee Willie Winkie with the faceless clock under his arm. The clock has no hands, because Willie, and the Dosser too, belong to a wonderful world that is timeless.

CHAPTER SIX

Sparrachat

A WINDOW SEAT

See me, Ahm a sparra – tha's right, a burd, a wee burd. Naw, no' a lassie. Kin ye no' see my feathers? Ye kin tell by ma accent that Ah come fae Glesca. That makes me a Glesca sparra. Ah don't mind that at a'. No' a bit. Mind you, if Ah really wantit tae blind ye wi science, Ah could tell ye that ma full Sunday name is *Passer Domesticus*. They tell me that's Latin, by the way, but it's no' much heard where Ah come fae. Well, imagine bein' stuck wi' a name like that aboot the streets. 'Haw, Passer, dis yer Maw know yer oot? Come oan, Domesticus, gie us yer patter.' Naw, I think I'll stick tae 'Sparra'. It sounds dead right fur me. An' anyhow, Ah've got yased tae it. So there it is, but.

The name Ah hate is 'speug'. It's the kinna name they gie tae yokel burds fae the country, it's no' right fur a Glesca keelie, bricks an' mortar burd like massel. Ah mean it's the kinna sound ye get as ye're gonnae throw up, is it no'? Naw, Ah don't like speug. Ah don't mind 'chookie-birdie' but. Ah sometimes get that fae wan o' the auld grunweemen when they throw oot the stale breid fae their windaes in the winter. But they

85

don't break it up enough fur wee yins like us. Ah sometimes feel as if Ahm tryin' tae get my beak roon a hale pan loaf. Mind you, we'll eat maist anythin'. Well, we'll gie it a good try any road. Ma mither ay says ye can gie anythin' a peck that ye see lyin' an' if it disnae bite back, ye can ay try a wee nibble. The thing is no' tae eat too much o' anythin'. Ay, she's a wise auld burd, ma mither.

She brought us a' up under wan o' they tenement roofs, ye know, where the rhone pipe meets the gutter juist unner the slates. There's ay a nice wee bend in the pipe there, know whit I mean? Ay, well, ma faither built a right cosy wee nest wi' grass that they goat fae the fitba' park and a bitta straw fae the cairter's auld stable. No' that it's a stable noo, mind. A fancy motor's there noo, but there's ay a bit o' straw fae where they used tae feed the hoarse. At any road, ma sparra-da made a fine wee place fur us aw, ma wee brother, Chappie, who wis the baby, then me. Ma mither ca'd me Cheeky, 'cos she said that's just how I looked when I came oot o' ma shell.

Even oor ain mither couldnae say we wur beautiful. We hid grey caps oan oor heids, black breists an' peely-wally faces. That's because we were toon burds, an' no' a bit like the country burds like the lark an' the thrush and the nightingales an' a' that poetic lot that wid never be seen deid oan the side o' a tenement wa'. Ah mean the grunfolk talk aboot an exaltation o' larks, know whit I mean? An' a murmuration o' starlings. God, they hivnae heard the racket the same starlings make oan a' the buildings in the city centre some nights. As for a murder of crows, Ah could well believe it. We wur aywis telt tae keep away fae thae craws, 'cos they wid sooner pit a beak in yer eye than pass the time o' day, so they wid. As for a parliament o' owls? Who says? They got the name o' bein' clever just because they never said or did anythin'. They've goat insomnia or something, fur they stey up a' night, sittin' oan a high branch staring wi' they big eyes intae the daurk. Whit's wise in that? They might as well be in their bed, like the rest i' us. Although Ah must say, Ah've never seen an owl in Glesca, but then Ah've never steyed up a' night eether.

Ah wonder whit they'd ca' us in they burd books? A twitterin' o' sparras – that sounds aboot right fur us, know whit I mean? We're no' much fur gawn aboot in gangs or flocks or walks or musters or whatever book-word they come up wi'. We ay like tae keep oorsels tae oorsels. The mair folk ye hiv aboot ye, the mair chance o' arguments an' bother. Ye see it wi' they geese. Silly big things they ur tae, ay squawkin' at each ither, an' aw at the same time. Nae wunner they get loast at times, the racket they make. Seagulls are the worst. They don't even talk oor language. They've goat bits o' patter they've picked up roon aboot the boats an' they shriek at each ither as if they wur sweerin' aw the time. They could only be ca'd a quarrel o' seagulls. Am gled ahm no' wan o' them. It must be awfy cauld sitting wi' yer arse in the cauld watter maist o' the time.

As for the pigeons, the doos, they're the worst i' the lot, so they ur. They're the scaffies o' the burd world. They never dae a haun's turn fur anybody, yet they strut aboot like lords, waitin' tae be fed on crumbs or whatever it is the grunfolk buy to feed them. Ah've seen them waddlin' roon George Square as if they own the place. Folk shouldnae feed them at a'. Let them scrounge aboot like the rest of us. They'd soon know whit it is tae go hungry, fur Ahm sure they've aw furgoat how tae forage. Right enough, there's the homin' pigeons – they're decent doos, different somehow. They earn their keep, but maist pigeons ur parasites. Them an' thur flat feet an' thur big fat bellies. Layaboots. Nae wunner they're made intae pies by the grunfolk. Am all fur pigeon pie.

Thank God naebody's thought o' sparra-pie. Ah don't think there wid be much feedin' in it. We're juist a wee baw o' feathers roon a bit bone an' gristle. Ay, but there ur advantages in bein' wee. Then again, maist o' the grunfolk in Glesca are wee tae, know whit I mean. Mebbe that's how we get oan, by the way. Sparras ur like aw toon-folk, we like it aboot the doors an' the windaes. There's aywis a crumb tae pick up. The auld grunfolk ur ay good tae us, although the weans kin be a bit cruel at times, but then they're juist bein' weans. They don't know oany better, dae they? Ay, so as Ah say, we like tae keep tae oor ain faimilies alang the rhone-pipeline, just like the grunfolk ablow us. Ye hiv tae know who yer freens ur if ye live in Glesca. Ach, but we ay get by.

Anyhow, Ah like it in oor nest. It his feathers a' roon the inside. Ah've nae idea whose they wur, but they wurnae oors. We hid haurdly enough to cover oorsels, never mind the wa's. It's a bit rough an' ready right enough but it's a cosy wee place tae come hame tae at the end o' the day, even though it's at the tap o' the buildin'. Ye must unnerstaun that sparras are hame-birds, by the way. Officially we're 'non-migratory' so they say, but that's juist a fancy name fur hame-buddies. Nae flyin' away every year tae the hoat places, like the South o' France, or Italy or *foreign* kinna places like that. Naw, we leave that tae the high-fliers, like the swallows. Ye know, the upwardly-mobile of the burd-world. Big ducks an' that. An' swans. It's no' fur the likes o' us wee fellas, but. I mean we'd never make it, wid we? Sometimes, Ah find it hard enough gettin' tae Glesca Green an' back, never mind trying tae cross the hale o' Europe. We hivnae the wing-power, ye see. We're made for the short hop.

Here, that minds me o' a wee hop Ah made that near wis the end o' me. Ah swear tae God. It wis wan o' they long, hoat days we used tae hiv in Glesca aboot the Fair, an' Ah wis juist kinna hingin' aboot in the still air, no' botherin' where I wis gawn, ye know the kinna feelin, driftin' like. When all of a sudden Ah fun masel' at an open windae. I'm no' right sure how Ah goat there in the first place. As Ah said, it wis that warm, an' everythin' was heavy in the efternin, like it is in summer. Thur wis haurdly a breeze in the air an' Ah wis gettin' by on low thermals Ah think. Ah wis trying tae keep masel' in the shade oot' o' the sun. That wis why Ah wis oan the daurk side o' the tenement and Ah wisnae watchin' where Ah wis goin'. The windows ur no' often as wide open – but then, it wis the weather, know whit Ah mean? Anyhow, afore Ah knew whit Ah was dain', Ah wis caught in a doon-draught, an' there Ah wis – inside – in the kitchen i' a hoose. An' that's a thing burds are no' supposed tae dae – least no' sparras. It might be a'right fur budgies an' canaries an' the like but the insides o' hooses is places fur Glesca sparras no' tae be.

But here, whit a palavar Ah set up in that room and kitchen. The grun-wummin let oot an awfy scream, which gave me the fright o' my life an' made me fly faster roon and roon the electric light hingin frae the rose oan the ceilin'. At her screamin', two wee grun-boys came runnin' in, and here, did no' the bigger wan run an' shut the windae, which meant Ah wis shut in wi' the three o' them. Ah made a breenge at the windae right away, but aw Ah did was bash masel' against the gless. Ah flapped my wings that fast they wur a blur. Aw Ah could till ma heart wis fair burstin' and the grun-wummin' wis greetin' an' the two grun-boys were laughin' like it wis great fun, but Ah thought Ah was done fur, so Ah did. Ah panicked. Ah needed fresh air, so Ah took a turn roon the room again, keepin' as high as Ah could tae the ceilin', away frae the big brush the wummin was wavin' at me like a mad thing.

'Open the windae, wan o' ye,' she wis shoutin'. 'A burd in the hoose is bad luck. Or a flittin'. An' we've only juist goat here. Yer daddy'll be mad.' Aw the time she wis thrustin' at me wi' the brush an' the grun-boys were having a great time runnin' roon the table an' pointin' up at me.

'Open the windae I tell ye.' The grun-wummin wis almost demented b'noo. I wisnae that jocose masel sittin' on the curtain rail above the bed recess. If she wis worried aboot bad luck, so wis Ah. Fur a sparra, there's nae luck aboot a hoose at oany time. Leastweys, no' aboot the inside o' wan. No' that it wis such a bad place, mind ye. It wis neat an' tidy an' the wireless wis playin' oan the sideboard, although ye couldnae hear much wi' the noise we were aw makin'. But then I saw them. On the wa'. Two ducks, wi' their wings spread oot, flying taewards the windae. An' here, were they no' nailed tae the wa', an' stiff as stookies. They were deid ducks, baith o' them. They must've burst in the wey Ah did, an' look whit happened to *them*. Ah hid tae get oot afore Ah wis nailed tae the wa' an' a'. Ah made a dart tae the mantlepiece an' got masel ahint the noke. Juist at that, it sounded oot the time wi' three big chaps. Ah thought ma hoor wis come, so Ah did, but I flew up again juist as the wee grun-boy's haun came roon tae get me.

'Mind the noke, oor Billy,' cried the wummin again. 'It wis yer granda's.'

Ah flapped my wings hard, an' Ah think that frightened the wee boy a bit fur he pulled back, and I flew tae the tap o' a big framed picture. It wis a man wi' a hat in his haun oan tap i' a big white hoarse, and Ah juist sat there, no' knowin' whit tae dae next. At that, there wis a loud knock at the ootside door an' the bigger boy ran intae the lobby tae see who it wis. Another grunwummin came bargin' in, a big fat wummin she wis.

'Ah could hear the racket ben the hoose,' she said, aw oot' a breath, 'an' Ah thought yer chimley must be oan fire or somethin.'

'Naw, Bella, we've a bird in the hoose,' said the first wummin and pointed at me with her brush.

'Is that aw?' said Bella, lookin' up at me. She had a nice face, the wummin, although she wis fat. 'Wid ye look at it?' she went oan. 'No' the size o' a curdy.'

Here, Ah thought, does the grunfolk's Bible no' say somethin' aboot two sparras bein' sold fur a farthin' – and that wan shall fa' doon. Well, that's no' gonnae be me, I thought, an' Ah dug my claws tight intae the widden frame. All of a sudden, the kitchen hid goat awful quiet and the four grunfolk were starin' up at me, an' I wis starin' doon at them.

'Ah can see its eyes,' said Tom, the bigger o' the boys, almost in a whisper.

'So kin Ah,' said his wee brother, breathlessly.

'They're juist like shiny wee bools.'

'Ay.'

Then thur mither spoke oot again. 'Is it bad luck, Bella?'

'That depends,' wis the answer fae the fat lady.

'Dis it mean a flittin', or a funeral?'

Bella didnae reply, she juist kept lookin' up. It wis funny, naebudy wis movin'. It wis as if we were aw feart we might break something if we moved. Ah wis feart awright, and I gave a glance ower at the two ducks oan the wa'. At least Ahm no' deid yet. Then Bella, the good neebur-wummin, took charge o' the situation.

'Right, yous yins. Oot intae the lobby the lot o'ye. Come oan noo, everybody oot. Tom, open that windae, son, as wide as it can go. We'll hae tae move quick afore the wee chookie-burdie up there shits aw ower King Billy. Yer man widnae like that, widdae?'

'Oh my God, so he widnae,' said the mother, hugging her brush tae hersel' as if it wis wan o' her weans, but she moved tae the door right away, her wee boy wi' her. Tom ran past them fae the windae an' wis first intae the lobby. Bella was the last. She stood at the door, then looked back up at me. Her face wis that nice as she said quietly, 'Right, my wee cock-sparra. Ye know whit tae dae. Away ye go then.' And she gave me the nicest wee smile afore she shut the door. Ah could hear her sayin' 'Shsh' then it wis quiet again.

Ah juist sat there, the panic runnin' oot o' me. It wis then Ah looked doon an' saw that Ah hid left ma mark oan the picture right enough. It wis a good joab the hoarse wis white. Well, Ah couldnae help it, could Ah? Anyhow, it wid wipe aff. Then Ah took a big breath, and kicked aff fae the tap o' the frame and in a great swoop I wis through the open windae an' intae the fresh air again.

Oh, it wis great, so it wis. Ah juist gulped it a' in and rose as high as Ah could, as high as Ah'd ever been in ma life, till Ah wis lookin' doon on aw the roofs ablow me. Glesca hid never looked mair beautiful. Honest tae God. It's a pity grunfolk cannae see the place fae whur Ah see it. It's aw laid oot like a coloured bedspread, the kind they have oan their beds. There's mair green than onythin', that's the surprise. It's aw the parks, ye see. Glesca's green and grey wi' bits o' black an' white. An' then there wis the Clyde, runnin' right through the middle o' the toon like a big grey-green, broon snake. It wis great tae look doon oan, Ah'm tellin' ye.

The higher ye get the mair ye see but I didnae want tae get above masel. I heard tell fae a sparra a coupla nests alang frae us that he wance flew tae Sprinburn Park an' it wis sae high there he goat snaw oan his wings. Naw, I know my limits, an' the East End'll dae me fine. Anyhow, I hid plenty tae see where Ah wis. Ah could see the streets, an' the people in them, an' the traffic. Ah could see the bridges an' the factories an' the schools an' the fitba' parks. Ah could see the University on its hill away tae the west and the reservoir at Milngavie tae the north an' the fancy Burrell Collection away tae the south. It wis like the hale wurld wis under ma wing. Then there wis aw the church spires and the towers. Aw 'man-made', as they say. An' aw the libraries, as many as pubs. Imagine hale buildins, juist fur books. Juist think o' aw that learnin' ready an' waitin'. As I glided high in the sky, I thought tae masel, the grunfolk hiv made a' this an' mair in a vast grun-space where the sea meets the sky and forests touch the mountains. Ay, there's nae doot, grun-man's a clever kinna species. He can dae aw sorts o' things, marvellous things, but there's wan thing he cannae dae – HE CANNAE FLY. He's stuck tae the grun, that's how they're caw'd grunfolk. Ah might juist be a wee stupid sparra, but Ahm a burd an' Ah can take tae the sky whenever Ah feel like it. Wi' that I gave a wee bit chuckle tae masel an' soared even higher. *Passeridae – Oh ay-ee!* Right enough, this beats bein' nailed tae a wa'.

Then, efter a bit, Ah could feel the light go. It wis the slightest thing but it telt me it wis time to get hame. So Ah let masel glide down nice an' slow in the late efternin sun tae where the rhone-pipe met the gutter and where Ah knew there wis eywis a place ready fur me. Instead, Ah haurdly goat my beak in the nest afore ma mither wis oan tae me fur bein' away sae long. She was sure the cat had goat me. Then ma faither, when he came in, gave me a right bollockin' for landin' in somebody's kitchen. 'We might be hoose-sparras,' he chirruped, 'but that disnae mean we live in hooses. There are plenty o' parks in Glasgow if ye want tae stretch yer wings. An' anither thing, where's the feedin' ye were tae bring back tae yer mither? Ah thought sae. While you were dain' yer interior decorating, we were foragin'. Well, there's nae supper fur you, my lad. That'll learn ye.'

It wisnae the welcome Ah expected.

Efter that, Ah wis leary o' open windaes. But Ah minded whit my faither hid said aboot the parks, an' whenever Ah hid the chance, an' the forage wis in fur the day, Ah headed out fur the wide, open spaces tae see whit Ah could pick up in the wey o' extras like bits o' vegetables an' stuff like that fae the allotments, an' the better class o' insect than ye usually get about the back courts. Ay, parks wir great.

We don't want fur parks in Glesca. There must be fifty o' them at least. Ah know, Ah've goat relatives in maist o' them. Faur-oot cousins in Rouken Glen, an' ithers nearer – but they don't speak tae us. They stey by Alexandra Park, which is in the East End tae, but they think they're a step above us because they hiv their nests in redstane tenements like Kennyhill Square an' no' in Parkheid greystanes like oors. They're that disappointit they cannae lay golden eggs an' hivtae be content wi' speckled just like the rest i' us.

Oor park wis Tollcross Park an' it hid everything as far as Ah could see, big trees, wee bushes, plenty o' grass, wide-open spaces, neat wee paths, hills an' even a runnin' burn gone through it. Ah could play masel aw day there, when Ah wis younger like, sometimes kiddin' oan Ah wis a big eagle soarin' ower the mountains, or a peacock walkin' wi' giant steps oan the bowlin' greens. Daft things like that. Ah just enjoyed the freedom o' the place, an' at least it goat me aff the streets fur a while.

There's eywis auld grunmen in parks. Auld grunmen in flat caps oan thur heids. Thur rheumy eyes missed nothin', an' thur noses ay hae a wee drip oan them, an' thur white moustaches wur ay yella wi' pipe-smoke. Ay, auld men wi' spittal that wis as vital as thur grip oan life. Ah wis nearly caught a few times. Ah mind though Ah hid a laugh wan time wi' wan o' them. Ah wis perched oan the end o' his bench an' he wis bletherin' away tae his mate, anither auld grunman, and Ah hopped a bit nearer so that Ah could listen. He wis talkin' that low that Ah could hardly hear'm so afore Ah could stoap masel, there Ah wis, up oan his shooder right at his ear, as bold as ye like an' quite perjink. An' dae ye know, he didnae gie a budge, but juist gave me a wee look an' went oan chattin' away. An' Ah juist perched there, quite the thing, an' no' a bit feart. Wisnae that great? It wisnae till he took anither draw o' his pipe that Ah nearly choked wi' the smoke an' hid tae fly aff quick juist tae get ma breath back. Ah looked fur that auld man many a time, but Ah never saw him again.

Other times I was near hit by a ba' when the boys were playin' fitba', so I tried tae steer clear o' the pitches when games wur oan, even though

I liked the colours o' the jerseys. It wis anither kinna colour among the bushes at times. Blushin' red might be right for some o' the things I saw an' heard fae my branch up above them.

'My bloody zip's stuck,' wis wan unhappy cry, an, 'Ye'll hivtae mairry me noo,' wis anither, although I couldnae tell whether the grun-lassie wis laughin' or greetin'. Oh ay, ye hear an' see aw sorts o' things fae the air Ah can tell ye, but Ah'd better no' say oany mair. Ye never know, it could get me intae trouble, an' anyhow, Ahm no' a nosy burd. I don't stick my beak in where it's no' wantit.

It wis Tollcross Park that hid the big hoose in the middle o' it. An' there wis this kinna exhibition in it wi' a stuffed deer caw'd 'Bobby'. Ah heard that he'd bin runnin' aboot the park no' long since. Well, so Ah heard. They hid forbye a big gless case fulla stuffed burds, wid ye believe? Ay, thassa fact. Ah didnae like that. Ah mean, who wid want tae get stuffed? But that's whare Robin Redbreast wis, ye know, Cock Robin, him in the nursery rhyme? Ye'll hiv heard it:

Who killed Cock Robin?
'I', said the sparrow,
'With my bow and arrow,
I killed Cock Robin.'

Ah wish tae protest, so Ah dae. There's nae proof that wan i' my lot knocked him aff, by the way. Ah know it wisnae me. That wee fly mighta seen him die, bit naebody goat a gander at who actually did it. Ah cannae believe that wan o' mine wid dae sic a thing. Ah mean, we're no' killers, like some Ah could name. We're no' even fighters, even though we're fae Glesca. Anyhow we widnae hae the strength tae haud a bow never mind shoot an arra aff it. Ah mean, Ah'm sorry he's deid an' that, but that Cock Robin wis ay full o' hisel', know whit I mean? Cock o' the walk, an' aw that. Him an' his wee rid waistcoat. He thought he was juist the thing. He wis oan the Cooncil, ye see. He wis that type, oan the committee for this an' that, an' he strutted aboot in that stuffy, pompous wey he hid, up tae his oxters in self-importance, so he wis. Aw because he wis supposed tae be brought back to life wance by St Mungo. Well, he's deid noo, an' no' even St Mungo kin dae oanythin' aboot it. Probably hid it comin' tae him, by the way. Politics, n' that. Know whit Ah mean?

And all the birds o' the air,
Fell a-sighing and a-sobbing
When they heard the bell toll
For poor Cock Robin.

That's a lie fur a start, by the way. There wis nae sighin' or sobbin' in oor nest. Or oany ringin' o' bells neether. But here, that minds me o' anither wee sparra-story. It was the bells that minded me.

It wis wan Hogmanay efter the bells, or mebbe it wis afore, Ah cannae mind. It disnae maiter. The grunfolk hid shut themsels up in thur hooses, it bein' that cauld fur it wis winter. An' there they aw wur, watchin' a box in the coarner that shows pictures. 'TV' Ah think they caw it. Burds can see it through Glesca windaes fur Glesca folk don't like shuttin' their blinds at night. Ah think they're feart they miss somethin'. Well, any road, wan night they were kickin' up sic a racket that Ah couldnae sleep, so Ah wings it doon fae the nest tae their windae sill an' his a keek-in. Sure enough, there they wur, sittin' in a semi-circle as if they wur hypnatised or somethin', while the wee grunfolk inside the box wur talkn' tae them or singin' songs or dancin' up an' doon.

At times, through the windae, Ah've seen the grunfolk greetin' at the songs, but this Hogmanay, as Ah remember, they wur greetin laughin', if ye know whit Ah mean? Ah tried tae see whit wis causin' aw the commotion but Ah couldnae see right because o' the hauf-curtain they hid at the windae so Ah flew up oan tap i' a big milk boatle and keeked in again. Ah just hoped naebody wid see me 'cos Ah didnae want tae get caught inside like afore, so Ah cooried doon as best Ah could an' tried tae see ower aw the heids.

The picture oan the box wis showin' a big, skinny, funny-lookin' grunman who wis hauf-singin', hauf-speakin' a song an' aw the folk in the room watchin' were killin' themsels laughin'. An' here, wis it no' a song aboot a wee cock-sparra. Ah didnae like the thought o' them laughin' at wan o' ma ain, but aw the same, Ah wantit tae hear whit it wis aw aboot. Ah had heard thur wur poems aboot nightingales, songs aboot larks, rhymes aboot cuckoos, even verses on hens but Ah'd never heard a song aboot a sparra. Well, here it is, juist as Ah heard it:

The wee cock sparra sat on a tree,
The wee cock sparra sat on a tree,
The wee cock sparra sat on a tree,
Chirpin' awa as blithe as can be.

Alang came a boy wi' a bow an' an arra,
Alang came a boy wi' a bow an' an arra,
Alang came a boy wi' a bow an' an arra,
An' he said, 'Ah'll get ye, ye wee cock sparra'.

The boy wi' the arra let fly at the sparra,
The boy wi' the arra let fly at the sparra,
The boy wi' the arra let fly at the sparra,
An' he hut a man that wis hurlin' a barra.

The man wi' the barra came ower wi' the arra,
The man wi' the barra came ower wi' the arra,
The man wi' the barra came ower wi' the arra,
Sayin', 'Dae ye take me for a wee cock sparra?'

The man hut the boy tho' he wisnae his farra,
The man hut the boy tho' he wisnae his farra,
The man hut the boy tho' he wisnae his farra,
The boy fairly glower'd, he wis hurt tae the marra.

An' a' this time, the wee cock-sparra,
An' a' this time, the wee cock-sparra,
An' a' this time, the wee cock-sparra
Wis chirpin' awa' on the shank o' the barra.

Ah didnae know the big grunman that wis singing oan the boax a' they years ago, but he wisnae fae oor street any road. Ah didnae stey tae hear any mair. Ah hid been oot late enough, an' anyhow Ah couldnae wait tae tell Chappie that we were famous noo fur we had a song aboot us oan the TV. But here when Ah goat up tae the nest again, wur they no' a' sleepin'.

Settlin' in beside Chappie, Ah pulled my wing up ower ma eyes but juist before Ah fell asleep Ah fun masel singin' tae masel:

An' a' this time, the wee cock-sparra.
Wis chirpin' awa' on the shank o' the barra...

I hid tae laugh. It mighta bin me.

CHAPTER SEVEN

Alice in Barrowland

IN ANOTHER WORLD

IF I CLOSE MY EYES, I can see the face of Central Glasgow staring right at me. It's a broad face and it's not always easy to take it in at a glance, but if you look long enough you can see it quite clearly and, you know, it's not at all that bad looking. You could say that the hairline extends from Maryhill to Balornock with the parting at Possil. The brow sweeps down through the northern territory of Springburn to meet the eyebrows. The left one as you look at it is the Botanic Gardens at the former BBC and the right is at Cowcaddens near Scottish Television. The bridge of the nose starts at Sauchiehall Street where it meets Renfield Street at Lauder's Bar, and runs all the way down past Central Station to its upper lip at the Broomielaw on the Clyde.

The river is the mouth and can be seen as a wide mouth or a big mouth according to your personal view. For me, it is a gaping mouth, always greedy for activity on its surface, be it ocean-going liners or rowing boats from Glasgow Green. As has been made clear in these pages, the River Clyde does all the talking for Glasgow. The city started by its side and has gone on from there ever since, and will do as long the water flows from the Leadhills and out to the Atlantic and the rest of the world. There is no stopping it and if it ever dried up, so would Glasgow. We thought it would decay when it lost its teeth, the shipyards, but it has recovered by other riverside developments like the summer River Festival, and, as a result, it's got its smile back. So it's miles better, as the famous slogan has it.

The prominence of its nose gives Glasgow its two profiles. Just like Buda and Pest, it's two for the price of one. Just as we are all born with our mother's profile on one side of our face and our father's on the other, so it is with a city. Going from east to west, you cross the bridge of the nose, as it were, and you see another face looking at you. On the left cheek we have Charing Cross and the West End and on the right we have Bridgeton Cross and the East End. What a cheek, you might say, to have two such contrasting crosses in the same city, but that's Glasgow. What is even more Glasgow, unfortunately, is that both places are not what they were. Charing Cross has been blighted by thoughtless road planning and Bridgeton Cross's cast-iron Umbrella wasn't protection enough against the loss of work and working people. So the cheeks might be said to be a little wan, but the years will surely bring a little colour back to them.

Govan and Parkhead are the ears and it's just as well they are apart. However, the sporting palaces they both boast show that their ears are close to the football ground. This is the new factory today and one where the ordinary working man is merely the fodder for the few who make the millions, but then, it was always thus and not even John Maclean or Jimmy Maxton could do anything about it. The Glasgow Eastern Area Renewal in 1976 only showed that houses didn't necessarily make homes. People make places to live in; ambitious, large-scale bureaucratic planning only makes for problems. Glasgow's still not quite 'in gear' in this respect.

If Glasgow's face had a beard it would hang, Jewish fashion, in two strands going down from Gorbals Cross and Govanhill and descending all the way to Giffnock. There's a stubborn chin beneath the hair and it has taken many a hard blow which ought to have knocked Glasgow out for the count – or at least spoiled her face, as they say in the street – but here she is, still on her feet, and still boxing. Benny Lynch was only one of many boxers from the Gorbals and he bravely took on the world even though it was much too big for him. It's a Glasgow failing.

So there you have it, the Glasgow face. The last thing to say about it is that it is heavily lined with streets, but then so would you be if you were over a thousand years old. These great thoroughfares began as cattle tracks then became dirt tracks and then cobbles and plane stanes until tarmacadam and asphalt gave us the streets we know today. These are streets, many of them, which I have known since I could first walk on them. I feel I know them all, and the ones I don't, I've heard of. I loved walking them and still do when I get the chance. I am an unashamed street-walker. That is, I have a pedestrian appreciation of urban architecture. I'm always on the lookout in any street in any city in any country, but I do love all the odd corners in and around Glasgow.

The Shipka Pass, off the Gallowgate, is just that – an odd corner. Even the name, taken from reports of the Russo-Turkish war of 1877, is exotic. Winding down to London Road, it was always *foreign* in my eyes, and up my nose too, for it was a Glasgow place smelling of spice, silks and carpets. This little thoroughfare might be considered as the start of my own Silk Road adventure in crossing Glasgow from east to west during my lifetime. In the Shipka, black and brown faces were added to dirty faces to give an Eastern allure to its turning staircase. I always found it difficult to relate it to Barrowland, which could be easily reached from either of its entrances.

Barrowland, or the 'Barras' as it is called, is just as colourful, but pure Glasgow – and pure dead brilliant at that. It's a bazaar (and bizarre with it), a multicoloured complex of trading carts, booths, buses and barrows, not to mention the tables laid out under the corrugated iron canopy where everything you can think of is for sale – at a price, and a bargain at that. It was here the patter was born, that swift combination of sales-talk and comic strip that sets the Glasgow stall-holder on a par with its best stage comedians. This is as it should be, for much of this three-ringed retail circus crowded into that Calton crush of streets between the Gallowgate and London Road is nothing less than theatre in the raw.

What had grown from an *ad hoc* collection of wheelbarrows loaded with oddments for sale became an assembly of carts and then a convocation of open lorries selling everything, including the kitchen sink. It has become big business and the resort of Sunday citizens looking for a bargain and free street entertainment. Unlike Paddy's Market down at the railway arches at the Briggait, the Barras doesn't confine itself to second-hand clothing but to moving everything and anything that can be bought or sold. Paddy's Market is the remains of an Irish self-help society whose day has passed, but the Barras continues to survive and thrive because it is what you want it to be – a treasure trove of bric-a-brac, a maze of possibilities where you might just find the last thing you think you're looking for, or just a good day out complete with hot dogs, fish and chips or the mandatory takeaway curry. It's a weekend wonder for some, and a nightmare of choice for others.

This Barrowland open-air market began in the early twenties when Maggie McIver and her family, who hired out carts to fish and fruit salesman to sell round the streets of the East End, bought a plot in the Calton and put all three hundred carts together at the weekend when the hirers weren't out on the road. Maggie was too astute to let any sales possibility pass her by so she loaded the empty carts with bits and pieces, much in the manner of today's car boot sales, and the Barras was born. Like any public venture, it has had its ups and downs, but now it is officially designated as the Barras Trust and recognised as one of the largest enclosed markets in Europe – a permanent, roofed structure, with its decorative gates, a thousand traders and a hundred shopkeepers spilling out into the nearby streets. It has become an enviable Glasgow institution and an indispensable part of its retail and leisure life. The sights and sounds of the whole world are here and it is all made to the customer's measure and pleasure. You can be sure of a laugh at the Barras, even if it is just at the enormous cheek of it. Anything can happen here, and it generally does. Fortunes have been made in these crowded streets and from some very unlikely beginnings.

There is the story of one Calton character who wasn't too bright at school and left as soon as he could. One of the first jobs he applied for was as a lavatory attendant with the Glasgow Corporation, but he didn't get it, because he could hardly sign his name, so he was thrown back on his own resources. He became a midgie-raker, that is, one who goes round all the back court middens to see what he can 'rake-up' from all the rubbish. It's amazing what people will throw out. In no time he had gathered enough to fill an old pram, and he wheeled it down to the Barras, where he took up a place on the fringe and sold his pram load of odds and ends in a morning. He returned the next week with another load, and so on until he had to hire a cart to take his rubbish, now called 'antiques', to the market. He eventually made enough to become a licensed trader. The McIvers didn't worry how shaky his signature was.

He went on to used cars, and then to car hire, and eventually to plant hire with the aid of Enterprise Grants and ended up a millionaire owning a trading estate on the Edinburgh Road. Even though he still had difficulty signing his cheques, he was by no means stupid, merely unalphabetic or dyslexic. He was never able to write more than his name. When an associate asked him what he might have been had he been able to write, he replied, quite truthfully, 'A lavatory attendant'. He never forgot that it all started for him at the 'Barras'.

Folk singer Matt McGinn was a friend of mine and a fellow East-Ender. Matt was a Calton man and he encapsulated in himself exactly what the Calton was: small in cubic area, rich in character diversity, full of fun, but ready to fight if need be, and not always fairly. As Matt said, 'Whit's a fair fight? If a man wants tae fight, there's nothing fair aboot it. The fightin' man deserves a' he gets – a bliddy good hidin''. Matt's song observations were merely a musical extension of his direct and pithy speech. If words were to be used at all, they were to be used well. It was the picture they set up that made it for Matt. Big words were for big thoughts, but a lot of wee words strung together nicely made for him what might be called 'a train of thought'. And Matt would puff away at his constant cigarette and tease out of his large mind a wee train that he would gleefully send on it its way by singing it to the weans in the street or to anyone else who would listen. Matt knew the Barras well:

> For Christmas he bought her a wee golden ring
> But later it made him embarrassed.
> He'd forgot the first thing
> That turned green in the spring
> Is jewellery bought at the Barras.

One of his songs also had a definite Barras link. It was called *Wullie MacNamara*. Note: This had to be read with a Glasgow accent.

> There wis a fella fae the Gallagate
> His name wis Wullie Macnamara
> An' the wey he earned his livin' wis
> B' ge'in shoart weight fae a barra.
> A wee fly man fae Charlotte Street

Has loast the place awra girra
He went up tae Wullie in the middle o' the street
Sayin' 'Hive ye goat eighteen-an'-a-tanner I could borra?'
Says Wullie: 'It wid cause me grief
An' even cause me sorra
Fur although I'm a very generous man,
I widnae gie ma grannie an oaringe fae ma barra.'
The wee fly man his the haud o' Wullie
An' he's shaken him tae the marra,
An' noo he has shaken his entrails oot,
He has thrown him oan tap o' the barra.
The polis are searchin' fur the wee fly man,
Though streets baith broad an' narra
Fae Glasgow Cross tae Springfield Road
Tae Parkheid – an' even farra.
The polis hiv gotten the wee fly man
They've pit him in the Black Mariah
An' he'll soon be up afore Langmuir
Fur causin' aw ris borra.
Noo, this is the end o' the sad, sad tale,
The sad, sad tale o' sorra
But I'll go oan writin' these rerr wee songs
An' I'll maybe hiv another good-wan-ready-fur-ye-ra
      morra.

Very sadly, one night in 1977, in his temporary flat not far from Byres Road, Matt tripped over the flex of an electric fire he had left on and hit his head hard on the fireplace, knocking himself out. The electric fire, meantime, set alight to his coat as he lay unconscious. So there was no tomorrow's song from wee Matt. It was a sorry accident but he has left enough songs to be sung in the streets for a while yet. And children will still skip to them. That's a real immortality.

Adults dance to a different tune and this was another area the McIver family catered for on their patch. It had been Maggie McIver's practice to give her hawkers a free meal with a drink and a dance at Christmas but when she couldn't get the hall she wanted one year, she built her own. The Barrowland Dance Hall opened on Christmas Eve in 1934 and featured Billy McGregor and his Gaybirds. Billy's band was as much of a concert party as a dance band, with the musicians doing comic turns and acts between dances. At one time, the Barrowland Ballroom vied with the famous Green's Playhouse, up town, as the mecca for dancers throughout Glasgow. The difference was that Barrowland had a roguish, even picaresque image and it drew the more raffish clientele.

This may account for the fact that during the Second World War it was almost another state of the United States. 'Go West, young man' is an injunction we all know from America's frontier days when a certain John Soule in Indiana advised American youth to look for Californian gold in 1851. Now young American servicemen in Glasgow were going in the opposite direction in search of something else, a treasure worth more than gold: Glasgow girls.

These city charmers were all fashioned from the same stock – a bright, bulletproof exterior encasing a stick of dynamite that always threatened to go off, but rarely did because buried deep down was a warm sentimentality. And wrapping it all up was an unfailing sense of humour. They found out early that a laugh could defuse the most difficult of situations so they got the giggles at every opportunity. They would laugh at anything – even if it was just at themselves. What those wartime nights must have been like for a young American far from home and with money and chewing gum in his pocket, one can only guess. The question was, who was chasing who on that dance floor? This was a Yankee at the Court of Queen Maggie McIver:

> There were so many sensations crowding in on him – the sheer pressure of the circus of bodies swirling around him, the tactile awareness of flesh under his hand, the sweat on his right palm that left its imprint on the back of her dress, the crackle of her taffeta underskirt that he could just hear above the sound of the band – a noise that made him think of other things. Things that he couldn't help, couldn't stop, or couldn't do anything about. It was hard to be reticent when her femaleness was right at hand, and when her perfume rose up from her neck and into his nostrils like the aroma from a harem, though it was probably a cheap scent. 'Gee, this was good,' he thought. It didn't matter that he could hardly understand a word she was saying in that Scotch

burr of hers. He just kept nodding and smiling. It gave him a chance to show off his good teeth. Wooed by the wail of the saxophone, excited by the squeal of the clarinet, they were pair-bonded in the circular trance of the slow foxtrot, all the slower because of the crowd. He tried to draw her nearer, but she knew how to use her elbows. But he, too, as a good American, knew his place and he'd never overstep the mark even if she let him. She could think what she liked but his thoughts were his own and they were becoming quite ungentlemanly. She must have sensed this because she stopped talking. Then both gave in to the music and the tension passed. Soon they forgot everything else as they wallowed in the strict-tempo, sensual atmosphere so closely engulfing both of them in that melee. Soon time meant nothing to either, other than the pulsing, mutual rhythm joining them together in the dance. Time would tell...

As indeed it did. Thirty years later, I was touring on the American Lecture Circuit with my Robert Burns solo, and in Akron, Ohio, I met Alice, an attractive, mature American matron who told me, as I signed her LP cover, that she came from Townhead and had met her husband during the war at Barrowland. Then she said, in that warm Scottish-American drawl, 'I was awful young then, but he was a great mover.' Then she laughed. 'And still is.' I could just hear the tinkle of Glasgow in her tone, like ice in a glass of Bourbon. She smiled and added as she left, 'He's a dentist.' I noticed that Alice had good teeth too.

By the time I met Alice, I was a part-time West-Ender in Hyndland. In 1967, I was living my weekdays in a flat opposite the tennis court on Hyndland Road while appearing in *This Man Craig*, and flying home at weekends for family life in Berkshire. This wasn't ideal for a father of three, as I was then, but I had to go where the work was, and for the moment it was in Glasgow. This was how I got to know the striving, successful professional Glasgow, which was mainly academic, dominated by the University on Gilmorehill; theatrical, keyed to the BBC at the Botanic Gardens and Scottish Television in the Cowcaddens; or artistic, with its centre at Mackintosh's School of Art on Renfrew Street and the Glasgow Art Club on Bath Street.

The Barras seemed a long way away now and my boyhood home in Williamson Street, or half of it at least, had already disappeared over the horizon. Oddly enough, the lane that I had once walked down to get to the River Clyde from our street in Parkhead was called Cairncraig Street – a conjunction of names that combined my own with the part I was currently playing, and the reason why I would be a semi-Glaswegian for the next two years.

I have very special memories of the Kirklee Hotel, which was then in Ruskin Terrace. Many of us used to meet there after a long day and swap stories – or lies. It was here I met a well-known English actor who told me that he had been asked to speak at a dinner, while he was rehearsing in Glasgow for an episode of *This Man Craig*. He was trying to make his posh hotel audience feel at ease, but the Home Counties plum in his voice wasn't helping him any. When he asked if they could hear him at the back of the room, an equally suave voice, but with a Glasgow undertone, answered at once: 'I can hear you perfectly well, but I'm quite happy to change places with someone who can't.' It's an example of the retort which is courteous and discourteous at the same time; that's very Glasgow. As was the spontaneous reply by a Glasgow singer, who was rung by a friend returning his call. 'You rang,' said the friend. 'U-tang,' was the reply. You have to think about that one. Think *King Kong*.

The other Kirklee story was told to us about the late Chic Murray, that tall droll from Greenock who was also a fine actor – when he bothered. It appears that Chic was awakened by a knock at the door of his flat by a gentleman who asked to see Chic Murray. Chic, being Chic, stretched to his six feet plus and, in his poshest drawl, informed the man that 'Mr Murray was not at home, but would you care to wait in the library?' The visitor beamed, impressed at such a facility's being available within a Glasgow flat. He made to step forward, but a large hand stopped him, saying, 'Fine. If you go back downstairs, turn left at the close, you'll find it on the corner of the next street. A lovely, big sandstone building, you can't miss it.' The door was then firmly closed. Chic Murray was *chic* indeed. His was a very special comic voice and one that is much missed. I especially remember his Jacques Tatti walk.

Street-walking in Glasgow's West End can be an unexpectedly rewarding experience. It's the detail that you catch that makes it worthwhile. An arch here, a doorway there, the shock of trees where you least expect them, the wealth of stained glass. Incidentally, a large contributor to this latter aspect of Glasgow's decoration was one John Cairney (no relation). And look out for the number of buildings that look back at you. There are house facades that have windows for eyes, doorways for noses, and mouths when the door is open. Many of these dwellings could be said to have had a facelift, and most are worth the bother.

There was a great deal of money in Glasgow at one time and what is left of it can still be seen within twenty minutes either way from Byres Road, and if the walk is tiring, you can put your feet up at one of the excellent little coffee houses that seem to be at every corner, the way pubs used to be in the East End. It's café latte country up west and Byres Road wears a French beret now and not a bunnet. After all, many of the area's churches are now given over to the worship of fine wines and to the appreciation of abstract art while others are made over to the service of local drama. It is obvious that the upmarketing of Glasgow goes on and much of it is happening between Great Western Road and Sauchiehall Street.

I made my last territorial statement in Glasgow a little further south when, in the eighties, my wife Alannah and I bought a second-floor flat on St Vincent Crescent in Finnieston, only minutes from the Kelvingrove Art Gallery in the West End. From our front window we could look out to the Finnieston Crane and across the river to the Garden Festival site, now all pretty houses and upmarket profiles. It was easy to imagine we were in Amsterdam or some other continental riverside city and not, in fact, only a few hundred yards from Yorkhill docks. The sweep of this superb crescent carries one well away from any pre-conceived notions of Glasgow.

As suggested before, this is Bath as Jane Austen might have known it, and only she could have been able to write about it today. The delicate minutiae of people lived in its lofty flats, lives so very different to the sea captains who once lived on these same top floors and pointed their telescopes out of these same windows to make a guess at good sailing weather. If the signs were fair, they would thump a heavy boot on the floor for the First Mate below to rouse the crew from the basement, who then crossed over what is now a bowling green to get their craft shipshape and ready to pull up anchor.

They went from here to the ends of the world and, in 1991, I went from here to New Zealand. I didn't know it then, but at the end of the crescent, under the new flyer, there was once a street called World's End. This was indeed the end of the world for me. The end of my two Glasgows – East and West. The first in the east, between Parkhead and Dennistoun – greystone to redstone. The second between Hyndland and Finnieston – red wine to white wine – and all conjoining to give an indelible picture of a four-square Glasgow that flourishes yet in my mind. It prompted the following play on words, or as I would rather think of it, some words at play.

> *D'ye mind*
> *When the sun seemed to shine a' day*
> *An' nights were storybook long*
> *An' ye made shadow-fancies on the plaster wa' o' the bed*
> *'til ye were feart o' yer ain imagination?*
> *But ye fell asleep afore the big monster got ye*
> *An' ye remember nothin' 'til the mornin'.*
> *D'ye mind*
> *How you woke fresh as toothpaste*
> *Eager to brush wi' the day*
> *That stretched ahead like a rimless desert*
> *Dotted wi' meal-times*
> *An' unexpected oases to staun an' stop*
> *Just to look at somethin'?*
> *D'ye mind*
> *When life was so big a thing,*
> *Ye never even thought about it*
> *An' if ye did*
> *It was only to giggle about how easy it all was?*
> *Now, you've grown up*
> *An' the world has shrunk a wee*
> *Takin' its simplicity with it*
> *Leavin' ye to fathom*
> *The complexity of the wrinkles on its tired old face.*
> *Your eyesight's not so good*
> *Ruined by politic short-sightedness*
> *The need to see what ye think ye have to see*
> *Missin' everythin' essential*
> *In your desperation to miss nothin'.*

D'ye mind
When ye understood nothin'?
An' ye see now it was a gift
An' ye threw it away.
D'ye mind?

Perhaps Glasgow is indeed a state of mind: a different way of looking at things, but never at a distance. Glasgow is right there, straight in your face, daring you to blink first.

CHAPTER EIGHT

The One, True Religion

A FIFTY-FIFTY BALL

THE MOST CRUCIAL QUESTION one can be asked in Glasgow is 'An whit school did ye go tae, then?' I have no doubt at all that most people in Glasgow have been asked that at some time in their lives and they are well aware that there is no educational curiosity in it whatsoever. Its purpose, first and last, is to find out your religion and class you accordingly, whether as majority Protestant or minority Catholic. This demarcation may not be as polarised today, but generally speaking this was the common view for years. Which was the reason why the questioner was anxious to determine your place in the Glasgow divide. In other words, on which side of the barricades do you belong?

This is all the stranger when one considers that Glasgow itself is a religious foundation instituted by a Catholic saint. The tiny candle of Christianity lit by Kentigern/Mungo kept its light throughout the Dark Ages and illuminated the building of an imposing Cathedral on the slope leading up from the Molendinar Burn to what is now Cathedral Square. St Mungo's Cathedral was built, or rather re-built, in a whole series of extensions from around the early part of the twelfth century. The first actual date was linked to Bishop Michael in 1115, which sounds more like a time of day rather than a calendar year, but the first confirmed working date was the dedication of the mortared stone church in 1136, so it was certainly an ongoing project.

For over one thousand years, Catholic practice was accepted as the norm before the Reformation during the sixteenth century turned Christendom on its head. A Presbyter was put in charge on behalf of the new Presbyterian Church of Scotland. From then on, Catholics had a bad time of it in Glasgow. An Anti-Popery Society was founded in the city and it flourished. The number of Glasgow Catholics swiftly diminished to a mere handful so that they had little need for their impressive cathedral. Their pastoral needs could have been accommodated in a room and kitchen. Before long, the statutes held it illegal to be a Catholic in Glasgow. This was to be at the root of so much evil in the future. St Mungo's, however, remained a cathedral, and has done so to this day, despite the fact that the Archbishop of Glasgow no longer has his *cathedra,* or Chair, there.

I must say this never occurred to me when, as a St Mungo schoolboy, I clattered down John Knox Street on my way back to St Kentigern's from school dinner in the Barony Church hall in Cathedral Square. Once again, the good Protestants were feeding the needy Catholics. St Kent's was the St Mungo's Academy annex in Duke Street at that time, bang opposite the high walls of Duke Street prison. We would sometimes wonder who was serving the stiffer sentence; the female inmates across the road, or us boys with Brother Michael for a double period of maths. My schooldays were spent at the historical core of my city but I never took much notice, even though the original Molendinar Burn dripped from a pipe in the wall on to our concrete playground under the shadow of the Great Eastern Model Lodging House for Men.

A prominent non-Catholic High School in our time was Allan Glen's, which was established in 1853 at North Frederick Street and Cathedral Street (later at North Montrose Street) as a private school for the sons of tradesmen and artisans. This hardly anticipated the late Dirk Bogarde's reluctant enrolment at the school in the thirties. Dirk told me, while on location in France for *Ill Met by Moonlight* in 1956, that he hated the school only a little less than he hated Glasgow. Maybe that was only because his schoolmates called him 'Derek'. They thought he did the school a disservice in his recollections of his Glasgow time. I always thought it a bit odd that Allan Glen's, a Protestant establishment, was adjacent to Cathedral Street and our Marist school looked out to John Knox Street.

The oldest school in Glasgow is Hutcheson's Grammar, which began in the Gorbals in 1650. Since then, other good schools such as the High School and Glasgow Academy were founded, but we never knew anyone from Parkhead who attended either of these. Catholic boys of any promise from all over the city went to St Mungo's at Townhead, or the 'Wally Dishes', which was our irreverent name for St Aloysius College at Garnethill. I went to the Mungo, principally because it was non-fee paying and because that was where most of my pals went Ultimately that was the deciding factor.

Catholic girls had the choice of Our Lady and St Francis at Charlotte Street on Glasgow Green, which, like St Mungo's, was available to girls all over the city. Notre Dame, on the other hand, was highly selective. The nuns there saw to that. Posh Protestant girls went to any of three good schools for girls in that same sector – Laurel Bank, Park School and Westbourne, all of which were a long way from our ken.

The first resident Catholic priest in Glasgow, Father Alexander Macdonnel, didn't arrive until 1792. He was followed by Fathers Forbes and Scott, from Enzie in Banffshire. Note that these priests were all Scots. The Irish priests, who were to become synonymous with the Roman Catholic clergy in Glasgow, didn't come until the Great Hunger a century later. Since I was a product of that same clergy at St Michael's Primary and St Mungo's Academy, it was obvious on which side of the fence I belonged, and it was also assumed that I supported the Celtic. And why not? They were a Parkhead team.

But they were more than that – they were an Irish team, and what was even worse in many Glasgow eyes, they were a Catholic team. And that was the rub. When a Glasgow man says 'Celtic' he means 'Catholic' and when he says 'Rangers' he means 'Protestant'. Celtic FC was the brainchild of a Marist brother, while Rangers was started by the McNeil brothers, who were members of a rowing club on the Clyde. One of the four McNeils, and the first Rangers captain, was called Moses, but that didn't make them Jewish, did it?

In the beginning, there was no religious association as such with either Rangers or Celtic, despite the fact that Celtic was founded by

Brother Walfrid of the Marist Order. The religious association did not occur until much later and soon became widespread, not only in football. At least the sporting link allowed a more tactful approach than 'Are you with us or against us?', which is what the original question really implied. Such blatant polarisation is a nonsense in the modern world of global warming, babies with AIDS, suicide bombers and the possibility of terrorist attack.

Yet in Glasgow there are some who still hold that the most significant date in British history was 1690 when a little-known Prince of Orange, a Dutchman, but then King of England because of his marriage to a Stuart Princess, a Catholic, defeated the Jacobite forces of the rightful King, James II, at the Battle of the Boyne. King Billy's image on horseback features prominently on banners at the Rangers end during football matches, and in many Glasgow homes too, yet these same people ignore the fact that King Billy and the Pope were political allies at the time, and that prayers of Thanksgiving were offered in the Vatican after what was regarded as a victory for Papal intentions. However, this irony is lost on many. Such historical facts have no place in the minds of the largely mindless.

For them, such facts give way to the preferred fancies and the silt of untruth builds up over the years. The cancer spreads into every aspect of their lives and colours their attitude to everything. Even the Scottish Football Association was tainted by the same brush, when Sir George Graham, the SFA Secretary, advised Celtic to remove the Irish tricolour from display at Celtic Park. But Sir Robert Kelly, the Celtic Chairman, resisted strongly. In this, he was assisted by the Rangers Chairman, who sensibly proferred the view that, if Celtic had broken no rules in flying the flag, they could not be disciplined by the SFA for continuing to do so. Celtic won this particular battle, but it is to be remembered that they did so with the help of the Rangers Board.

It is unfortunate that such example given at the top level was not always heeded by the minority of fans at the lowest level. I had my own experience of this when attending an Old Firm match at Ibrox. I was amazed to see that a section of the Rangers support, seated at the edge of their particular compound, spent the whole game mouthing unprintable obscenities at the nearest section of Celtic supporters who were similarly fenced off a few metres away. Their retaliation was limited to a resigned, 'Aw, fuck off,' but the barrage of abuse went on, with the abusers paying no attention to the match at all but chanting their ghastly slogans into the green and white scarves nearest to them. The Celtic reaction, or lack of it, only drove the blue-and-white horde to even fouler excesses of the tongue, spat from cheeks red with rage and flecked with spittle. It was an ugly sight and it has stayed with me. The tragedy was that none of the baying section could have been older than fifteen – mere boys. Where did such hate come from? You could see it in their eyes. Even when Rangers scored, the venom never abated. Instead it was an excuse to hurl even more invective into the air. This kind of juvenile savagery surely went deeper than a football match. Let me hasten to say that, in this respect, it is not only Rangers supporters who are at fault. Celtic, too, have their hard core of irrational bile which is just as ugly.

At the time of writing, the Rangers Board is making strenuous moves to eradicate the chanting of sectarian songs and other aspects of hooligan behaviour at their ground. Celtic, too, are following this lead, although it has to be mentioned that their support did win an official award from FIFA for their sportsmanship following Celtic's defeat by Porto of Portugal in a UEFA Cup Final, and the same FIFA fined the Rangers club for the singing of sectarian songs by their support. However, FIFA did accept that this had been going on for so long in Glasgow that it was recognised as the norm for such Scottish sporting occasions. Even neutral supporters are open to the effects of the unwarrantable prejudice it has fostered. Most real supporters of any club are not hooligans or thugs and they lament as much as anyone the actions and the chanting of their forgettable few. But 'facts are chiels that winna ding', as that well-known non-Catholic, Robert Burns, put it. The bulk of decent Glaswegians, both blue and green, are the real losers. But it must be said that the blinkered determination to see only one point of view has strangled any hope that either side will move to bring about an armistice, let alone a lasting peace. A plague on both their houses.

However hackneyed this Rangers-Celtic rivalry has become, the result of it is that, in Glasgow, we are all inheritors of a sadly outdated conflict which holds everybody prisoner to a dead past. It's this sort of thing that gives religion a bad name, but it is a poison that persists. Despite the advance of sophisticated thought on both sides, the antidote has still to be found. Will it really require the move of the two clubs into the English Football League or will the hooligans of both sides carry their canker over the border with them? A more draconian solution might be that the teams combine as Glasgow United and take on the world – but that is a scenario belonging to science fiction. It is noticeable that one doesn't see many turbans among either support, or any kind of coloured face for that matter. Support for these massive clubs has long ago ceased to be local. It is worldwide, and the sickness travels.

I was in Canada not long after the 1971 Ibrox Disaster and took part in a fundraising concert for the families of the victims. This was held in Hamilton, Ontario, and I appeared with my old pal from Drama College, the late Andy Stewart, a well-known Rangers fan, but still a great friend. I wrote a poem for the occasion and recited it in the show. I remember the first line was 'Speaking as a Celtic supporter...' I remember well the hush that descended on that huge audience as I spoke but they heard me out and at the end one man came backstage to ask me for a copy of the piece. I gave him my only copy, written on hotel notepaper and he thanked me profusely. Before going, he said, 'You know, John. You're the first Cath'lic I've ever spoke tae.' He was a quiet, well-dressed middle-aged man, another successful Glasgow exile, but he actually said that as he shook my hand and went away happy. I was quite bewildered.

The main trouble with the Rangers-Celtic-Protestant-Catholic wrangle is that its roots, on both sides, lie with a cadre of particular families. Some are born to the condition and learn to live with it. Others pick it up by contagion at the street corner and others have it thrust upon them by nothing more than peer pressure at work where it is risky to be thought the odd man out. Whatever the case, the bias is deeply ingrained. Vague half-truths have been handed down from generation to generation, so that spurious attitudes have hardened into gnarled postures which cannot be questioned. A pedigree of pernicious libel has inculcated a hate of the other side, which is often stronger than the love of their own.

It was the First World War that sparked all the old controversy into new flame. Ulstermen were imported from Belfast's shipyards to work in the Govan yards of Harland and Wolff and they brought with them all their Orange baggage – including their mistrust and fear of all things Catholic. Celtic became an immediate focus for a built-in hatred and all the anxieties of the earlier Irish invasion were revived. Where before the issue had been entirely economic, there were now cultural and religious differences, which fanned the flames of suspicion and mistrust and led to the division between the two factions. As I have said, much of the old animosity has been dissipated in our more complex times but there is still an acrid atmosphere when these clubs meet, a hangover in every sense, but suggesting a folk memory that lingers like the smell of smoke and wet ash after the blaze has been extinguished. It can really get up your nose.

Yet this was not always the case. Rangers were the invited opposition in Celtic's first ever competitive match in 1888. Celtic won but it all ended with a supper for the two teams at St Mary's Hall in Abercomby Street and a singsong round the piano. If only that could be the case today.

Officially, both clubs are appalled at the continuing situation but trimming the branches won't do much good – the roots go down too far. The trenches of bigotry may be crumbling, but they were dug deep and both sides are still wary of lifting their heads above the parapet. They still have to tread warily. Here we have a situation where two sets of Scots, two sets of Glaswegians, two sets of football supporters, draw back into themselves and away from each other to create a wholly artificial gulf, which is entirely insupportable by actual historical fact, but which, nonetheless, survives. Supporters still go by their separate buses to their segregated enclosures and celebrate or drown their sorrows in their designated green or blue pubs, as sacrosanct to the respective congregations as any mosque or synagogue is to a Muslim or Jew. Are we really to believe that a man's spiritual views are to be ascertained by his reaction to an inaudible air played on an invisible flute or that a young man's football future can be determined either by his name or by what school he went to?

Of course, such rivalries are not only true of Glasgow, other big cities have the same problem. Belfast knew the same tensions between its own Celtic and Linfield, as does Liverpool today with Everton, and Birmingham City with Aston Villa. We have the two Manchesters, United and City, and in the north-east, Newcastle United and Sunderland. In North London, there is Arsenal and Tottenham Hotspur, and so it goes on. Each of these couplings represents the same face but with very different expressions. One always holds itself to be the older, the more established, and the other, the challenger. As the saying goes, it is a game of two halves, but in this case, it's the 'haves' and the 'have nots' that are vying. There is something of the same religious undertow in some of these rivalries, except that in Glasgow's case it is the driving force.

Partisanship is inevitable in sport. It is the element of opposing forces that gives any game its drama, but it is rarely based on religious denomination. If the 'Old Firm' of Celtic and Rangers represent the mainstream religions in the city, the other Glasgow teams might also have their place as occasions of worship. It is often forgotten outside Glasgow that there are other teams in the big city. It takes faith of another kind for followers of these clubs to make their presence known in the football world. Queen's Park, the Gentleman's Club, and the oldest in the country, still attracts its quality support. Clyde, those 'bully wee' guys, recently transplanted from Shawfield to Cumbernauld, fill a necessary need for those who prefer neither blue nor green, and Partick Thistle are really a rule unto themselves, but still provide thrills at Firhill for their hardy cognoscenti. Their passion is in their zeal for their respective clubs and not for any tribal causes.

The basic fact is that football in Glasgow is not about religion: it *is* the religion for so many of its citizens. It is what inspires them most, what brings them out of themselves and lifts their thoughts to higher things. In short, it does what religion used to do in a less secular world. Even football terms had a religious ring. In the first years of the game, football had its 'Scotch professors', mainly Glasgow men, players who found gold in their boots as missionaries for the sport in other lands.

One of the earliest was John 'Jake' Madden, nicknamed the 'Rooter' because he once uprooted a goal post with a ferocious shot. A boilermaker in the shipyards, he was an unashamed professional footballer when that status was illegal. He played for Dumbarton and Celtic in their great days but in 1905, at the age of forty, he was given the chance to coach in FC Slavia-Prague in Czechoslovakia. His best friend, Jackie Robertson of Rangers, was originally offered the job, but then decided he didn't want to leave Glasgow, so Jake borrowed Jackie's blue jersey and had himself photographed in it as a Rangers player. The Czechs were happy to accept him at face value and Madden set out for Prague to teach football. He married there and was to remain in Czechoslovakia for the rest of his life. When he died he was given a state funeral and buried as a national hero. Not bad for a boilermaker. It was said that as his Czech improved his English deteriorated but, as a Glasgow man, he always insisted he never could speak English anyway.

Jackie Robertson did follow Madden to Europe and brought the game to Budapest in 1911 and, in due course, this resulted in the famous Magyar side of the post-Second World War era which repaid this original Scottish tuition by trouncing England at Wembley. Other missionaries in the early part of the twentieth century were McKean who took soccer to Germany, McNab and Muirhead, whose mission lay in the United States and others like Harley, Dick and Cameron spread the gospel in South America – where Brazil comes from. All these coaches were Scotsman on the make – but look what they made. A worldwide sport, a language understood by all nations, because it's mostly spoken by the feet. It might be described as the Esperanto of the kicking world.

As a spectator sport it has always been the obsession of the deprived, which is why it blossomed in Brazil. It was much the same in Glasgow, but Glasgow venerates all its sporting heroes. Especially its boxers. Why is Benny Lynch, the boxer, still a legend? Because he looked, in his prime, a typical Glaswegians of his inter-war age – under-sized, under-rated and over-ambitious. Benny took on the world and won, and was dead gallus with it. But then he couldn't beat the demon in himself and he died of the drink at thirty-three. Peter Keenan, another champion, had more sense, and became a promoter. Jim Watt was the last Glasgow world-beater in 1979, but even if all these men were lightweights, none was a pushover and I bet nobody ever asked any of them about their schooling. A quick uppercut might have been the reply.

Why *are* all Glasgow's world champions boxers? I realise that a Sumo wrestler would have been highly unlikely but why have we never produced an Open Golf Champion, a Wimbledon winner or an Olympic swimmer? The answer is that golf and tennis were pastimes for the well-to-do and the water in the Glasgow Corporation Swimming Baths was always too cold to encourage aquatics. Glasgow is essentially a working-class city and it attends the needs of a proletarian population. We have our golf clubs and tennis clubs of course, even several successful cricket clubs, but for the great multitude it is football alone that draws them out and brings out the best – and worst – in them. It has the elemental conflict of boxing, the tension of golf and the finesse of tennis, and attending the game demands the stamina of the swimmer. Added to this, the big match has all the fervour of the revivalist meeting. What more can a poor man ask from any sport?

As the son of a poor man, I first saw football from the bottom of the pile and its innocence then reflected my own. I must confess that, for me, a match-day Saturday was as holy as any Sunday. Even more so, because it was a Holiday of Obligation. I was obliged to attend Celtic Park, and I regarded it a serious mortal sin if I missed a home game. One grows out

GLASGOW BY THE WAY, BUT

of this holy zeal but it is pretty intense while it lasts. My dreams were unashamedly woven through green and white hoops. We would never have thought of wearing these jerseys ourselves. That would have been sacrilege. You had to *earn* the right to wear your team's colours, and you certainly couldn't buy that right by paying seven pence at the Boys' Gate.

Nowadays, the purchase of a jersey is almost mandatory for supporters of every club, but that's because it's all part of the contemporary marketing strategy. To me, it is the merchandising of something very precious, but that's just another sign of our material times. It's another thing we have to live with. Fundamentally we are still the people, but for us, football is more than the people's pastime – it *is* us, in thought, word and deed.

Once upon a time, the working man stoically froze on the terracing watching his team through the haze created by the hot air steaming from a thousand mouths around him. It was primitive but passionate. It was football not only as a religious alternative but as social therapy and a balm to a drab weekday existence. For the great mass of the people Saturday was bright yellow – a day to be savoured whatever the weather. To see the local football team running on to the park was the working man's defiant reply to a helluva week. He was happy to leave the outside world at the turnstiles and come into his own among his mates.

Most of the cloth-capped, non-descript army of other-ranks were factory hands but on a Saturday afternoon they could forget the foreman and be their own boss for ninety minutes. It wasn't much time out of a working week, but it was invaluable, and life-giving. A good win on a Saturday helped a man face the furnace or the workbench on a Monday morning. If they lost, what had really changed? There was always next Saturday. There is *always* next Saturday because there is always hope. You might have the faith but you need the hope, and charity you leave to the Salvation Army. The greatest lesson learned on the terraces is that you never know. Whatever the pundits say, no game is predictable. But then, neither is life, thank God.

Euripides, talking of the spectator at the first Olympiad, described him as: 'A man of loose tongue and intemperate manner, given to tumult and to leading the populace to mischief with empty words.' He might have been speaking of any Old Firm supporter. Yet appearances can be misleading. Feelings run deep in and around this game. The Tartan Army is still on the march, and however ludicrous their simian antics look swinging from goalposts in their long tartan skirts and outsize tammies, they can still beat their bare chests with a pride that owes more to Tarzan than tartan and sing 'Flower of Scotland' as if it were the 'Battle Hymn of the Republic'.

Yes, 'We arra peepel' they might bellow raucously. And for an hour and a half they are. To many, the football experience feels like the one, true religion in the very broadest sense. Then let us pray that come it may that we will witness together the universal feast of football:

> On rectangle altars of grass
> Between the perimeter white lines
> Set like commandments on the green field,
> The champions parade
> Like hirsute high priests in gladiatorial motley
> To concelebrate their lithe liturgy
> In temple playgrounds
> Under a canopy of lights
> Or in the glare of sun at the peak of day.
> In vast cathedrals open to the sky
> The initiated hordes
> Banked on the heaving terraces,
> A mound of heartbeats,
> Meet to give worship upon the appointed day
> In this, their most accessible shrine,
> Making a multi-coloured congregation
> Of all the peoples of the world,
> Who gaze, as with one eye,
> On the carpet of ever-changing patterns
> Where the chosen acolytes pursue their rites
> In camera,
> And for a whole world's notice.
> Playing the game, the selected few,
> To whom is due
> The homage that men once gave to gods.
> New gladiators give of themselves
> As they relive for others
> The pain, the fear, the excitement
> That primitive hunters felt in ancient days

In the dark forest or desert plain.
Now,
See how
The new tribes gather.
Spectators,
Participators,
A nameless laity chanting their disjointed hymns
To raise young godlike men
In their own image, as man-like gods
To praise and give honour
To the solemnity of men at play
So that all who see might wonder
And, in a golden moment, know a lifetime's dream.

Alas, that kind of passion is all but spent, but it is not quite dead. Other forces might now be at work in the game and corporate interests may seem to have usurped the people's loyalty and dedication, but at the roots, at grass level, football is still football. There was a time when men who never wept in their lives cried at a football match. Whether they were tears of joy or despair hardly matters, the fact is they were moved to deep emotion and were not afraid to openly express it; something they would never do in the outside world. This is why football is important to more than half of Glasgow, even today. But they need to be re-inspired. The hooligan dirt still sticks. The game needs to be washed clean. A total immersion in real values. Bring back the old time religion – in the football sense – and restore the faith of all those genuine football fanatics who live in Mungo's city. There is no place for rationality here. It is no less than the re-awakening of a dream.

Glasgow possesses three football grounds that might be considered as iconic temples to the modern game. Hampden is the national stadium, Ibrox is home to Rangers and Parkhead is Celtic's ground. Each of these is a sumptuous palace of the people's sport, the very latest in stadium design. They can seat nearly 200,000 spectators between them and the tension created by even a third of such numbers in a prescribed, canopied space can generate enough energy to power the overhead lights. In what the poet Dan Wilton called 'this barking, mongrel town, where Scots and Irish coalesce', the football playing field may have levelled out somewhat, but the goalposts haven't moved. As Robert Louis Stevenson has pointed out, 'There are chalk lines.' And they still apply – whatever school you went to.

Yet the real excitement, the joy of it, is in the sense of anticipation before the game. That remains for the present-day crowds just as much as it did for their fathers and grandfathers. The game's still beautiful, the rules still apply and the old fervour still hangs in the air like incense.

CHAPTER NINE

Speak the Speech

AS I WAS SAYIN'...

'YOU'LL NEVER ESCAPE from your rabbit warrens unless you can talk,' explained Mr Bennett, our English master at St Mungo's. 'You can't get out of the ghetto until you have the password – and that word is English. You've got to learn to speak it clearly, think it thoroughly and use it effectively.' Old 'Billy' Bennett, who *was* English, was determined that we pimply fourth-years should be equipped with the only tool that would help us dig our way out of the pit that, as growing Glaswegians, we were in – a command of the English language as she is spoke and writ.

Despite Mr Bennett's semantic evangelism, it could not have been an easy matter to try and teach young Glaswegians to 'speak properly'. How could we, born as we were with a lazy tongue and a mile-wide glottal stop? Bennett's English period was an attempt to increase our vocabulary and was in no way meant to be an elocution class. Anyway, we wouldn't have known what to do with a 'brown cow' and we would've spat out 'a bool in the mooth'. We could speak film-American better than we could Queen's English, the reason being that we were as much educated by films as by any school. Besides, we were mostly tenement boys, and tenement boys are not trained to table talk. They know street-corner chat but small talk is not their forte and big talk is for con men. For tenement boys, talk is not a social skill – it is a weapon, or at least a defensive shield, and must be used with discretion.

We were more used to being talked at or down to and we weren't encouraged to take the conversational initiative. Perhaps this is why so few Glaswegians became public orators. It is often difficult for them to put their thoughts into words but that doesn't stop them speaking their mind. In this context the risk is a pronounced use of a certain four-letter Anglo Saxon expletive as a utility word. Even though it is an accepted obscenity, Glaswegians have been able to put it to expert use as a noun, adjective or adverb – and often as all three at once, which is a high skill.

St Mungo's Academy introduced me to boys who came from other places around Glasgow, such as Johnstone, Bishopbriggs, and all those outlying 'villages' that make up the Greater Glasgow conurbation. To me these boys seemed like aliens. Like us, they didn't speak correct English, but they did speak slightly differently. Rather than streets or roads, their addresses were lanes and terraces, and that must have had an effect. Gradually, however, all these voices melt together in the playground and we arrive at the asphalt *patois* that goes for school-speak in any city.

John Kirk from French Street was a talker, and real star material. After attending St Mungo's, he pursued a career in insurance in New York and Toronto, married his boss's daughter and shot up the office ladder. He was scheduled for great things in the business world but died of a heart attack just as he was about to fly to Dublin for the races. He always loved the horses, as did his dad. This fact helped John win a commission during his National Service in the army in 1948. When interviewed by the Officer Selection Board, John explained that his lack of scholastic documentation was due to his home being bombed during the Clydeside Blitz – as had his school with all its records. When then asked what his father did, John replied in his best manner, with his Glasgow voice at attention, 'A King's Messenger, SIR.' The Board was duly impressed and John received his commission. What John didn't tell them was that the king in question was not George VI, then on the throne, but William King, the bookmaker from Bridgeton, and Mr Kirk Senior was one of his runners, who operated from the back of a Brig'ton close. Yes, John Kirk was a Glasgow boy; and boy, was John Kirk Glasgow-smart.

John and I were both street boys but there were 'road' boys, 'drive' boys and 'avenue' boys at our school and even one or two that were 'garden' boys, but they were rare. There are only two boulevards in the whole of Glasgow, one in Mosspark and the other in Knightswood, but nobody from there went to our school. These thoroughfare labels may have merely been a change of address, but they count because they determine accent and attitude. Generally, streets were at the lowest level. Roads weren't much better but you were a tiny step up if you lived on a drive or an avenue. 'Gardens' in your address lifted you well into the land-owning class (by our standards). The word itself had the sound of things superior in it, even if it were merely in the intonation. Anyway, boys who lived in 'gardens' didn't shout as much we did in the streets. They had no need to: they lived in quiet areas where a loud whisper would have disturbed the neighbours and a shout would have brought out the police.

The only sounds there were footsteps crunching on gravel or someone's piano practice heard through an open window. Similar sounds were also heard from the windows of drives and avenues but to a lesser degree. We 'streets' lived in a different world: we shouted all the time and piano practice was unheard of. We were able to run up our concrete stairs, three at a time, yelling the initials 'O-P-E-N' at the top of our voices so that our mother would have the door open just as we arrived on the landing. We had no inhibitions up the close.

The young Glaswegian is trilingual. He has a voice for the house, a voice for the school and a voice for the streets. The first is the one he was born with, the one he learned at his mother's knee; the second is imposed on him by his schoolteacher; and the third he picks up for himself on the street. He soon learns to keep these various voices in their different compartments. He would never use his street voice at home and would certainly never use his school voice in the street. Our primary teachers were mostly Irish-Glaswegian like ourselves but they insisted that we speak as well as we could, even if it was only to answer our names for the register. 'Present, Miss' had a certain ring to it when you might have preferred to answer with a grunt.

Our real language was street-speak. This was the one you learned quickest because your survival depended on it. Obscenities were assimilated almost naturally and very often a ten year old in the tenement tribe had a command of curses that would have gratified a well-travelled sailor. However, it was also true that the more a boy read, the less he swore. I can only guess that this was because he had glimpse of another and better vocabulary. At any rate, we donned our triple vocal armoury very early but with no great sense of which to use when for best effect.

Some boys were known to erupt with street-talk at primary school and bring a blush to the woman-teacher's face. By the time we were at secondary, we had more control and, in any case, some of our male teachers, then just back from the Second World War, would have given back just as good as they got, with six of the best added just for good measure. So we had to watch not only what we said, but how we said it. On the whole, the best tactic was to say nothing.

Yet we liked to chat. We even enjoyed the occasional serious discussion. As young boys in the street we had a fondness for night-time sessions in our back-court wash-house. We would light the fire at the old boiler and put a lit candle at the window to show the neighbours that a meeting was in progress. This was a puerile debating chamber: a boys' parliament dealing formally with street problems as children saw them. In this way we would deal with those of our age who got out of order or give a hand to anyone who was in bother. It was our washhouse Witan.

Sadly it all came to an end when, late one evening, my father came down to the back-court and dragged my brother and me out of the wash-house, telling us it was no place for a couple of healthy boys to be at that time of night. He should talk. We had to pull *him* out of the pub every Friday night. Jim and I didn't think it was a healthy place for grown men to be either. So that was the end of our wash-house sessions, which was a pity. I only wish it had occurred to me to keep minutes. What reading they would make now. All I know is that the instinct to talk among ourselves was there from the beginning, as was the reluctance to agree. It seems to be a Glasgow trait.

For me, debate proper began in my student days when, during my first Christmas break, I was frog-marched by my mother to the local Labour Exchange to sign on for casual employment at the 'Student Counter'. Most students were sent to help sort Christmas cards in the George Square Post Office but in that first year, 1951, I was put on a lorry with about a dozen others and driven along Old Shettleston Road to a wood yard where we were dumped into the hands of an unsuspecting storeman, who didn't know what to do with us. 'I only asked if somebody could gie us a haun,' he said, bewildered by the large posse of adolescent bodies standing in front of him.

It was then I suggested to the wee man that if he gave me a bit of paper I would take down everybody's name and at least it would look official. He could then put us into pairs and allocate the various jobs he needed done, such as sawing, breaking up sticks or stacking the wood on to the lorry. The storeman looked relieved. 'Good idea, son. Ah'll get ye some paper.' He disappeared into the hut-cum-office and I persuaded the rest of the boys to form a line. They did so because they were freezing just standing there and they were glad to have something to do. The permanent employees of the yard, three older men, looked on in open derision. 'Is it Fred Karno's army we've goat?' asked Delaney, the tallest one, loudly. I could see he might be trouble, the big man.

In no time, I had the names on the page and the wee storeman had sorted out the work pairings. Everyone had a job – everyone except me. I was left standing there with the storeman, so he said, 'You'd better come in wi' me, then,' and he pointed to the hut. 'I've just put the kettle oan. Whit's yer name then?' I told him. 'Right then, John, we'd better get in oot the cauld.' It certainly was cold and I was glad of the electric fire in the hut, never mind the hot cup of tea. As I sipped, I watched the steam rise from my fellow-students' mouths as they sawed and cut and stacked and lifted. I learned an important lesson that day: the importance of the clipboard in the workplace and the effectiveness of a show of action, even if it only amounts to taking down names.

At lunchtimes, we all crowded into the one shed that had a heater and ate our sandwiches. I noticed that the permanent workmen stayed apart from the students as if they were a different species, although the only real difference between us was that we had got our Highers and they hadn't. Arguments used to spring up and fights could have started, which is when I had my other idea. I asked the three workers if they would like to take part in a formal debate the next day against three students. They were a bit dubious but on the nod from big Delaney, they agreed. They actually seemed a bit shy. Never mind, I went ahead and set things up in the big shed during the lunch break.

I took my subject from the leader of the storeman's *Daily Express* that day. There had been fighting in Egypt and British troops were fired on at Suez so, being 'in the Chair', I offered the following motion for debate: 'That this house deplores the British presence in Egypt.' Following some discussion about the use of the word 'deplores', the workforce took this on and the students argued against. I was astonished at the rough eloquence of the three workers, especially Delaney, who put his points over pithily and with humour. On the other hand, I was ashamed of the patronising attitude of the three students, who couldn't keep the superior smirk out of their voices as they spoke – but they were drive and avenue types so probably couldn't help it. After half an hour, the motion was put to the vote of the other students in the shed and the workers won on a show of hands. The three of them cheered and jumped up and down as if they'd just won the Scottish Cup, and from then until the end of the holidays, I chaired a daily lunchtime debate.

It showed me just how powerful the latent voice of the average Glaswegian is. Coated as it is in dust and debris, it tends to sound laryngeal even when perfectly healthy. Because of the dry, husky tone you can always tell a Glaswegian in the dark. The voice you hear rarely goes deeper than the tonsils and even then it is not encouraged to linger. The diaphragm is a region unheard of and the head voice is something you get with a cold. Any projection would be thought pretentious. This is why it's so breathy and always sounds as if it's being forced through clenched teeth.

No, the Glasgow voice is not a thing of beauty. Which is why there is a heavy reliance on the nod and on a certain vocal response which can only be written as 'Uh-huh'. The accent, too, sounds lugubrious and the tune of the inflection is often funereal, yet it is one found often in press circles and behind the bar in most capitals around the world. The Glasgow barman is one of Scotland's most successful exports along with a certain, awkward kind of politician. Who knows, by the time this book is in the shops, we may even have a Glasgow Prime Minister? Gordon Brown is a product of its University, even though he was Rector of Edinburgh as a postgraduate. I am sure he would have regarded that as missionary work.

In my youth, the unofficial meetings of the St Michael's Boys' Guild took place at the Bank of Scotland corner near the public lavatory at Parkhead Cross. Here, we would brag and show off to each other, offer daring views on everything and generally challenge the world. We were in our twin-toned teens, with breaking voices to match, and just itching to get out and get to grips with life. Standing on a corner was almost the only occupation open for working-class men for much of the twentieth century and it was then inherited by their sons. Their grandsons now resort to chatrooms on the Internet but, before these cyber times, standing on the corner was our main leisure recourse. It was rarely boring for the whole, broad pageant of street theatre took place under our close scrutiny, and the broads often stole the show. Bird watching had a whole other meaning in Parkhead.

It was at this same corner I first realised Billy Bennett's hopes for me and deliberately spoke English for the first time. That September morning, I had auditioned for the brand-new College of Drama about to open at the Athenaeum on St George's Place (now Nelson Mandela Place). I had not long finished my National Service in the RAF and had a vague idea of going to university, even though I had already been a professional actor with the Park Theatre before being called up. Suddenly this new Drama College sprang up and I thought it would provide the academic outlet I would need, while at the same time train me properly for a career on the stage. So I applied for an audition and was told to report to the Athenaeum Theatre at ten o'clock the following Monday morning.

The first thing the English voice from the darkness of the auditorium asked me was what was wrong with me. 'Have you a cold?' it called out.

'No.' There was a pause, then, 'Do you sell fruit?' I was perplexed and didn't know what to say. Then I realised that he thought I was a barrow-boy, a street trader, and that my natural huskiness was a result of vocal exertions in the open air. What it was, of course, was the normal, inhibited utterance of the street boy. Somehow, I got through Hamlet's 'Advice to the Players' – 'Speak the speech, I pray you...' – and I was in. I think they accepted me as a student less for any innate acting talent I might have shown but more for the vocal challenge I offered. It was one of the sins of belonging to Glasgow. However, one of the first things I was told was that if I ever hoped to make a living in the theatre I would have to get rid of my Glasgow accent. And this was the reason I had to take the plunge that night at Parkhead Cross and speak in English.

'Whit time's it?' asked one of the boys. I took a deep breath.

'Twentee-minutes-too-nyin,' I answered all the way from my diaphragm.

All the faces turned to me as if I had spoken in Serbo-Croat.

'Whit's wrang wi' you, then?' was the general tenor of enquiry – politely translated. I tried to explain but it was futile. Their banter swamped me and I retreated as fast as I could with shouts of 'Romeo? Wherefore art thou Romeo?' following me down Springfield Road. At home, I retired to my room and opened my brand-new textbook, just acquired that day: Clifford Turner's *Voice and Speech in the Theatre*. I never stood at the Cross again.

In Parkhead, I was made to feel as if I had betrayed my origins because I had suddenly decided to speak 'proper', as they put it. I had let down my class by aspiring to middle-class ambitions. Next thing I would be buying a house and a car. I might even be tempted to vote Tory. Looking back, I can't really blame them. In Glasgow, as in most places, the whole voice and accent question is a social thing. It all comes down to snobbism. It's not what you say, but how you say it that matters. There's a built-in superiority or inferiority complex, depending on which side of the tracks you came from. I was seen to be making a jump from 'street' to 'gardens' all in one go, and this was held to be presumptuous. How dare I be ambitious?

On 10 September 1950, I reported to the former Liberal Club (now a smart hotel) which was the site of the first ever College of Drama in Glasgow. I was one of the intake of twenty young Scots, the first to be trained for the professional stage in Scotland. However, the equivocal attitude to the theatre shown by my old Parkhead pals was typical: *'Hey John, ur you gaun oan the stage, then? Or ur ye juist actin' it?'* There was also the often-sounded view that it had also altered my sexual orientation because, in their eyes, only poofs or upper-class people from Giffnock or Bearsden became actors. It was a trying time, but I eventually reached a level of accent neutrality, which convinced producers in London years later that I was Polish. I told them it was Mansion Polish, but few of them got that. You had to belong to Glasgow.

The College of Drama has grown over the years to become the Royal Scottish Academy of Music and Drama with its own complex in Renfrew Street and today, in size and reputation, it may be said to rival the long-established Royal Academy of Dramatic Art in London. This would no doubt have pleased the man whose idea it was that Glasgow should have its own stage school – Dr Osborne Mavor, otherwise known as the playwright, James Bridie. Bridie, himself a Glasgow boy, knew the Athenaeum well, having founded the first Glasgow Citizens' Theatre Company from its stage.

Even as a practising doctor, Bridie was to go on to write many fine stage plays but he might also be well remembered as the man who made YGORRA ('You've got to...') part of every Glasgow student's rag day slogan, said while rattling a collecting can in front of passers-by. Another product of Bridie's Edwardian studenthood was his kind of vocal Glasgow-ness – where 'dark' was 'derk' and 'park' was 'perk' and every vowel was constipated. This was the other Glasgow voice, the West End 'Kelvinsaid' accent, favoured by those who lived west of Charing Cross, and it couldn't have been more different to our sluggish, slurred, East End delivery.

James Kelman, author of the 1994 Booker Prize-winning novel set in Glasgow, *How Late it Was, How Late,* does not dwell long in the West End in his fiction. He goes right to the core of Glasgow-speak where it has all its verve and vitality: in the factories, pubs, and on the streets. He tells it as it is today, with no holds barred. Kelman is a Glaswegian, but he is also a good writer, and however dour and sour his language might appear on the page, this is a genuine Glasgow voice, and we had better believe it.

Let's face it, the common language in Glasgow is bad. Swearing has been raised to an art form in many quarters, especially the City Chambers, but the bowdlerised minutes of meetings have saved the councillors' blushes even if they make for less colourful reading. Factory dialogue is hinged on the use of *that* epithet and would hardly be understood without it. Coprolalia rules – OK? The only comfort to be taken from the Glasgow accent is that very often even Glaswegians can't understand each other. What is voiced in Easterhouse might sound incomprehensible in Whitecraigs – and vice versa. With the recent influx of genuinely foreign tongues, Glasgow may be well on the way to creating its own Babel if it doesn't sort out its vocal act. Will it be the case that the future Glasgow will only be known for sentences ending in 'but' and for an incurable polyglottal stop?

Even so, the voices will still hang in the air. And as long as there is a Glasgow, their sound will go on, echoing down the ages and reminding us that we still have the gift of the gab and that, whatever the accent, Glasgow speech can be erudite, compelling, challenging and endearing. However it sounds, if you mean what you say, then you'll generally say what you mean. Then you can say what you like – and how you like. If you speak from the heart, you're bound to be understood.

Real Glasgow crack, however, is none of these things. It is rough, crude and generally a pack of lies, but it *is* necessary. This is talk with style and panache although its vocabulary is hardly drawn from Oscar Wilde or Noel Coward. It is the language that begins at the closemouth and is carried on the steam from the wash-house, but a certain exuberance is added and it is this that gives it its vitality. It's what holds Glasgow together. Like the Irish *craic*, Glasgow crack is the basic, unifying fabric of its working-class society, calling for an expert arrogance by the man (or woman) holding the floor while at the same time allowing for a proper (and humorous) self-abasement on his or her part. It is bonding; a dance form in words; a sort of verbal GBH without prejudice; a mutually beneficial trading in insults where bullshit comes back as an intelligent truth.

At his own level the Glaswegian can vocalise con brio. Many citizens have 'the patter', as it is called, and it is this ability to swim with words at high speed – *vide* Billy Connolly – that is the characteristic of good crack. Once a session gets going, there is a tolerance of unfounded opinion as long as it's funny or interesting and allows the Glaswegian an expression of the fundamental generosity of spirit which underlies his excessiveness. In good crack you can never go too far. Political *in*correctness is mandatory. This modern obsession has no place in a convention where the sense of what is said is less important than the effect it has on the hearers. Good crack lives only in the moment and often won't bear retrospective examination. It is all in the NOW where everything real should be – and crack is *real*.

In its pub situation, it is an art form practised by consenting adults in public. Anyone can join in but there is a risk involved. You may hear more about yourself than you'd like to know in the blether as it rises and falls around the table. There is genuine articulation here as the human situation is explored from the ground floor up. Dr Johnson would be searching for words in this environment and Oscar Wilde would hardly get an epigram out, for there is no room here for decoration. Every conversational shaft is a spear to be used unsparingly with no mercy shown by either party. In the rowdy, smoky battle for attention, words must count; the superficial comment is just so much spilt beer. When the crack gets going, nothing else matters in this tutorial for the unlearned and closing time comes too soon on a group who have travelled together down the centuries in a couple of hours. They have come a long way from the day's petty lies and pompous pretences. Here, lies have to be outrageous if they are to be believed. These orators live by paradox and contradiction, both of which seem only too palatable in a state of semi-intoxication. However they are not intoxicated by the exuberance of their own verbosity, as the cliché has it, but by the very aliveness of the exchange as it happens.

Dr Mike Paterson is a New Zealander now living in Canada, who studied for his doctorate at Glasgow University. In order to navigate a safe passage through the seamier kind of Glasgow pub, he professed support for Partick Thistle, a particularly volatile football club in Maryhill. This won him immediate sympathy and entry into the world of Glasgow crack. Mike soon became an ardent devotee. Over a dram at our table, he told me what he remembered of it:

> Crack is a whole world away from e-mails and text-speak. It belongs to a literal freedom of speech where the inexpressible is expressed in clumsy metaphor but is nonetheless a warm, even heated engaging of like and unlike minds in a convivial situation of their own choosing. Body language is also spoken with effect. Signals are given among friends and strangers that tell of things behind the eyes and deep in the soul. They know there are more things on heaven and earth than fitba', TV and the wee burd behind the bar. Crack allows a man to come out of himself. Self-awareness is only possible through the awareness of others and it is all the 'others' that comprise this people's parliament, this platform for improvisational theatre, this vehicle for free-form poetry, this angel-speak called crack for minds that crave a spark to light the candle in their heads. If there's a good laugh in it, so much the better, but at least it will offer something to ponder during tomorrow morning's curried hangover.

They speak the speech, but, in the end, it's not what's said that matters, but how it's heard. We speak with the head but we hear with the heart. A good talker is always a good listener and there are many interesting listeners in Glasgow.

I once overheard a conversation which proved that M. Giles de la Tourette is still alive and well and living in Glasgow. This is a true incident. The scene is a fashionable café-bar just off Byres Road. Two youngish, well-tailored Glasgow men, sharp enough to be distinctive, but not enough to cut it, are seated at the bar. The taller member quaffs his glass of pricey Chardonnay the way his father would have downed a pint. The other watches in admiration. The tall one then puts down his glass sniffs, and then says very deliberately:

Tall member:	'See you?'
Small member:	'Aye?'
Tall member:	'See me.'
Small member:	'Aye.'
Tall member:	'We're fucked so we are.'
Small member:	'That right, Jim?'
Tall member:	'Fucking right, pal. The fucker's fucked the whole fucking thing, so he has. Fucked us up proper.'
Small member:	'Whit'll we dae noo then, Jim?'
Tall member:	'I'm fucked if I know.' (Pause) 'Same again?'
Small member:	(whispers) 'Sorry, Jim. I'm skint.'
Tall member:	'Aw, for fuck's sake. See you....'

I was sorry I had to leave at that point.

CHAPTER TEN

One Singer, One Song

BEST OF ORDER!

'A SCOT OF POETIC TEMPERAMENT, and without religious exaltation, drops as if by nature into the public house.' So said Robert Louis Stevenson in defence of Robert Fergusson, who died young, alcoholic and mad in 1774. If RLS is right then Glasgow has bred a large population of poets, given the number of men that could be seen in the streets leaning over at a very defiant angle to the pavement. Lucky for them, they didn't have far to drop to find a pub, as there was one at every corner in Glasgow. So much so that I was convinced, as a boy, that pubs were necessary to hold up a building.

This is no less so today, but even if wine bars have replaced the traditional corner public house, the pub still survives as a social centre. Formerly, from late Victorian times until the coming of television, pubs were the only interior alternative to the football ground for the Glasgow male and they served the same dual purpose of escape and inspiration. The local was the club, social hub, information kiosk and masculine pleasuredrome. Women were strictly barred. The late Cliff Hanley noted a sign in a Glasgow pub which said 'No Ladies Supplied'. 'I suppose,' quipped Cliff, 'you had to supply your own.' Only a certain kind of determined virago ignored the ban. She would gather her shawl about her grey locks and charge head first into that man's citadel to make a place for herself in the corner. Here she might spend the whole night over a glass of stout, or, in better times, a port and lemon. Occasionally, she might be joined by a pal of similar taste, and before long, publicans were forced to provide a place for the ladies, although they would never call themselves as such. They were referred to as 'Auld Biddies'.

Singing was not encouraged in case patrons might be inflamed by the rendition of party songs, of the kind that were never sung at parties. In the cloth-cap world of the masculine ghetto, coarse language was the lingua franca and a necessary supplement to any anecdote. The company of women would have inhibited this convention and prevented the drift into anesthesia which most men sought in public bars. Anyway, a man in his pub was his own man. He was free to have his say on any topic, although his ability to say it markedly diminished as the evening went on. He compensated by saying it louder.

This was why, by closing time, the noise from the pub was such that the wives in the nearby closes always knew when to put on their men's dinner for yet another reheating. The din of the pub's 'scaling' or 'timming' could be heard at the end of the street and many households would brace themselves for the weekly Friday night fight. Friday was pay day and the housewife's dread was that the publican would see more of her man's pay packet than she would. However, it was a typical post-pub incident that led directly to the writing of the song now universally recognised as the Glasgow anthem, although few stand up to sing it. Few can stand. The lyric itself is quite explicit in offering the picture of the wee Glasgow man at the very height of his self-esteem; which he only attained at weekends with the best suit on, a fag in the mouth and the price of a few drinks in the satchel, as he put it. It was then and only then, he was able to speak out and sing out as we all learned to:

> *I met wi' a few o' my cronies,*
> *Wan or two pals o' my ain*
> *We were in a hotel*
> *We did very well*
> *Then we came oot wance again.*

Then we went intae another
And that is the reason I'm fu'.
We hid twa deoch an' dorises
Sang a few choruses
Listen, I'll sing them tae you:

CHORUS
I belong to Glasgow,
Dear old Glasgow toon
There's somethin' the matter wi Glasgow
For it's goin' roon and roon.
I'm only a common auld workin' man
As anyone here can see,
But when I get a couple of drinks
On a Saturday –
Glasgow belongs to me!

There's nothin' in bein' teetotal
An' savin' a shillin' or two,
If your money you spend,
You've nothin' to lend,
Well, that's all the better for you.
There's nae harm in takin' a drappie,
It ends all your trouble and strife.
It gives you the feelin' that when you get hame
You don't care a hang for the wife.

The song has become accepted as the stereotype of the Glasgow drunk, but the irony is that it was written by a Dundonian. Will Fyffe was a successful Scots character comedian between the Wars who later made his name in London's West End, on Broadway, and through a string of black and white films. A first-rate actor, he learned his trade in his father's barnstorming company before the First World War. Jack Fyfe managed a troupe of players which travelled through Central Scotland with their portable wooden theatre presenting their Penny Geggies to whatever audience they could fit in a village hall, big house or barn.

Will, as the boss's son, played as cast, which means he performed as required by the management. By playing everything and anything here, there and everywhere, young Will assimilated the basics of acting from its very roots. He could not have had a better theatrical training. He learned quickly how to play a house; that is, to manage an audience. The actor learns best simply by 'doing' it: performing in front of people – strangers – who tell him soon enough whether he's got it right or not. Will Fyffe learned his craft from his audiences as the best actors do.

On the outbreak of the Kaiser's War in 1914, he left the family troupe to form a double act with Lily Bolton, his first wife. They called themselves the Fyffes, adding another 'f' to his surname: an idea he got from the famous brand of bananas. The act did not last long as Will Fyffe's métier was for solo character comedy. His character studies were, or appeared to be, *real*, only because they were so well observed. Particularly so with his Glasgow drunk, with whom he introduced the famous song. Even its genesis was real.

In the summer of 1919, Will was taking Lily and their two daughters for a day at the Clyde seaside and they were waiting on the platform at St Enoch's station (now no longer with us). Suddenly they were aware of a commotion at the ticket gate. The collector was having trouble with a wee Glasgow man who had taken a generous refreshment and was fumbling in every pocket trying to find his ticket. The collector, exasperated, tried to get some sense out of him. 'Well, where have you come from? Do you belong to Glasgow?' The wee man stopped suddenly and, drawing himself up to his full five-foot-four, intoned with all the over-enunciation of the drunk, 'No, sir. At this very moment, Glasgow belongs to me.'

This exchange stayed with Will Fyffe, and on the train journey he mulled it over. Staying true to tradition, he scribbled it down on the back of a cigarette packet and put it in his pocket. Before he reached the holiday destination, he had most of the lyric in his head, together with the tune we all know today. Not being a musician, he was unable to write out a top line, but he couldn't get it out of his mind. He tried to sell the song to fellow performers, as he never thought of performing it himself. Neil Kenyon, the Scots comedian, turned it down because he didn't belong to Glasgow. Nor did Harry Lauder, who was born in Portobello, but Sir Harry, an excellent comic singer, wasn't keen to sing a song extolling the virtues of alcohol. 'But what about your own "Just a Wee Deoch an' Doris"?' protested Will.

'Ah, that's different,' laughed Lauder. 'That was just one – and anyway, it was a wee one, ye ken.' So in 1921 the song went back into Fyffe's pocket. It was around this time that his wife Lily was drowned at sea on her way to join her husband in Dublin, so songwriting was put aside. He remarried in 1922, the new Mrs Fyffe being Eileen Pooley, a dancer in a revue in which they both appeared. By now, Will's career as a solo performer was going from strength to strength and the years passed successfully and happily. Then one day in April 1927, when he was in Glasgow preparing to open for a season in a new revue, he decided to take a day off to go fishing. As he was walking past the Pavilion Theatre on Renfield Street on his way down to Queen Street Station, the theatre manager, Jock Kirkpatrick, suddenly came rushing out from the front box office and grabbed him.

'Will! I'm in a real jam. My top of the bill has just cancelled and we're supposed to open tonight. We need a name to take her spot. Could you fill in?'

'Oh aye,' said Will. 'How long's the spot?'

'Quarter of an hour, maybe half an hour if it's going well. Could you manage that?'

'Oh aye. Do I get her money?'

'Of course. And her dressing room.'

'That clinches it,' grinned Will.

'Thank God. Let's have a drink on it,' sighed Jock.

And so it was decided. The fishing tackle was put aside and both men got down to business. Money was not the decider: at the time, Will was earning £600 a week as a top of the bill in London, but Kirkpatrick had a genuine emergency on his hands and Will couldn't let the man down. The only problem he had was deciding what to perform. He was under contract to do the other review and the script and music he was then rehearsing were copyright to that show, so he had to think of something different for Glasgow. What else but the nearly-forgotten 'I Belong to Glasgow'? He could ad-lib some patter around the song to fill in the spot. Fishing was quickly forgotten as the two theatre men sprang into action.

Fyffe still had no music for the song, so Jock summoned his musical director, the appropriately named Haydn Halstead, to 'write out the dots' for the band to play that night. Will had it all in his head, and in no time, there on the page was the song as we all know it. Oddly enough, some people think that Mr Halstead wrote the melody, but no, he merely set it down as Fyffe sang it over to him.

He had an attractive singing style but what was even more effective in performance was the patter material Will Fyffe delivered that night, virtually off the cuff yet in an absolutely believable Glasgow manner. All his well-honed skills of observation and timing, as well as the audience control he had learned on the road were brought to bear, so much so that a real drunk man appeared to have invaded the theatre and wandered on stage. It had all the impact of a star act with the underlying weight of a genuine dramatic performance. It was a sensation from the start. If he made the song that night, the song also made him. A London agent, Tom Pacy, was watching, and phoned his office to claim he had discovered the next Harry Lauder.

Not quite. Fyffe had come into his own and was unique. Just hearing him play with the word 'teetotal' made you realise you were in the presence of a great clown:

> When a man takes a drink, he's a man. But when you're teetotal...tee...teet't'l...Ach! [the disgust conveyed here is worth a whole speech in itself] when you're tee't'l [deploying the double glottal] you get the rotten feelin' everybody's your boss.' [He then gets on to the bosses, or the 'capistalists' as he calls them, in their motor cars, who] 'point their skinger of forn at the poor Glasgow working man going home intosticated. What's the poor fellow to do? He's got to get home.

This comment is heightened by his use of precise English. The social comment is within the laugh gained so it is swallowed painlessly, but the accent is strongly on the comedy: 'I may be under the affluence of incohol, but I'm not so think as you drunk I am.' What was so brilliant (as the drama critic James Agate pointed out), was that Will Fyffe played a drunk man trying to be sober, and not the sober actor playing at being drunk. It was great music-hall entertainment and also great acting.

What a loss he was to theatre. It would have been wonderful to have seen his acting talent stretched, as a Peer Gynt or a Falstaff, in a play that could have been produced somewhere like the Edinburgh Festival. Tragically, it was in the year of the first Edinburgh Festival, 1947, that Will Fyffe died as a result of a fall from a window at Russack's, the hotel he owned at St Andrews in Fife. He had been ill with mastoids in the ear, affecting his balance and causing him, while taking a telephone call on the balcony, to accidentally trip over the low balustrade onto the courtyard below. It was a fatal fall, made all the worse by being from the very height of his powers.

Sid Field was the only comedian who might have rivalled Fyffe in character work, and possibly Tony Hancock in his later years, but neither of these men could sing and they rarely came north of the border. Glasgow didn't have a good reputation among English comedians. The Empire on Sauchiehall Street was the variety house where English comedians 'died' and American crooners sang. When Des O'Connor walked out to face his first Empire audience, he was so unnerved he fainted. When Morecambe and Wise made their Empire debut, they were greeted by an unwelcoming Glasgow voice: 'Christ, there's two o' them!'

Even if it was the graveyard of English comics, the Empire itself was buried in 1963. On the theatre's last night the cast of specially-invited star guest artists joined the audience in singing – what else? – 'I Belong to Glasgow'. Did the ghost of Will Fyffe's original drunk man join in? He is still an anonymous immortal. I wonder if he ever heard the song he'd inspired being sung? The composer himself is buried in Sighthill Cemetery in the north-east of the city on the west side of Springburn Road, so, in a sense, he still belongs to Glasgow. But his song belongs to the world.

Yet any song sung in Glasgow, even today, has to be sung in a Glasgow way: getting the full value out of every note and stretching and bending the voice to extend the melody line as far as it will go. Generally, before the Glasgow singer pleases his or her hearers, he or she must please themselves. After all, they are their own best audience. Once in full tune they regale themselves with their own sound so that it seems as if they are singing through one, big, broad smile. They unwrap the melody from their person as if reluctant to let it go. Dead gallus, so it is. This is public singing as practised by footballers on the team bus or by the younger element at drink-fuelled family parties. You never hear it at dances. If you did, every dance would be the slowest of slow foxtrots. There is an unashamed indulgence about it, which by its sheer lugubrious pleasure takes it beyond the maudlin. Very often the voice is a good one, and the singer knows it – and he or she makes sure you know it too.

Glasgow singers are like great, plumed birds – they warble, playing on the melody line with an enviable ease. The highest praise a Glasgow singer can earn is to be called 'a great chanter'. 'Chant' describes exactly the wail that announces the start of every number; a siren that warns the listener to leave all musical susceptibilities at the door and give in to the *sound*. It is a broad, plangent tone and it tends to make the most harmless Tin Pan Alley ditty sound like an anthem. Glasgow singers 'never walk alone' – they drag their listeners along with them. They do every song 'their way' and make no bones about it.

This is why Glasgow is so sympathetic to American Country and Western music. It is the lied of the working class, and the sadder the story the better. When your own lot is nothing to brag about, it always helps to hear of someone who is worse off. The Devil may have the best tunes but in Glasgow they're done country style and your Glasgow singer does them full justice. All towns have their sounds and Glasgow's is Nashville, Tennessee as much as New Orleans is Jazz and Detroit is Rhythm and Blues. This is the reason that the Glasgow's own Grand Ole Opry stands so proudly across the Clyde from the armadillo Exhibition Centre. This is blue-collar Glasgow at its most tuneful. After all, we have a Dolly Parton and a Kenny Rogers up every close.

Every family has its 'rerr singer' and he or she can be relied upon to give their all at every social occasion from christenings to weddings and funerals. My brother Jim's party song is 'Moonlight in Vermont' crooned soulfully to himself for the most part, and to his own great satisfaction. Mine is the Irish folk song, 'She Moved Thro' the Fair', which makes me a minority taste.

I was a great admirer of Robert Wilson, the Newarthill tenor whose enormous popularity with Scottish audiences sometimes obscured the fact that he really could sing, and to the highest operatic standards. He was a heldentenor in a kilt and sporran and in his prime his power and control were awe-inspiring. Unfortunately (but much to the delight of Scots everywhere) his voice was continually heard in songs that hardly did his talent justice. He was always 'stepping gaily' by the edge of some loch, striding up a mountain side, being wistful 'down in the glen' and illuminated at all times 'by the northern lights of old Aberdeen', yet his was a voice that merited a spotlight at Bayreuth.

I first met Mr Wilson when we were both appearing at a charity function at the Glasgow City Chambers in 1951. He was past his prime but was still the singer and the perfect gentleman, with the slightly forlorn look of a man who was lost. He told me that he had taken the easy way in his career by yielding to the overwhelming demand for his voice in variety and light entertainment rather that testing it with the best in recital and *opera seria*. He remarked that 'for the serious artist, the easy way is always the wrong way. The right way is always harder.' I vowed to remember that. At that time, there was a possibility that I would sing for my professional supper and I was being trained to that end by Robert Wilson's own teacher, Eliot Dobie, whose studio was just off Great Western Road. Whereas the splendid Wilson voice was *tenore robusto*, mine was a rather tentative *tenore lyrica*.

I leaned more towards Canon Sydney MacEwan, the John McCormack soundalike from Springburn. MacEwan had first thrilled student audiences at Gilmorehill before attracting Royal favour in London and later, through his recordings, a worldwide audience who longed to hear the old Irish and Scottish songs so beautifully sung. Sydney MacEwan was the Glasgow voice in its Sunday-best, whose shoes shone as brightly as his scrubbed face. His gentle, refined, polished tones were made for the concert platform but they originated from up a tenement close but with a nod towards St Joseph's Catholic Church on North Woodside Road.

As an altar-boy, MacEwan got his first chance to sing in the liturgy of the Mass every Sunday, and no doubt the insider view he had of the priests at work led eventually to his own priestly vocation, which he discovered while touring in Australia. He elected to give up professional singing just as he was beginning to make a real vocal impact, but he chose to go with God instead. Obviously his taste was for altar wine and not ambrosia.

It is unlikely that MacEwan, for all his purity of voice, would have been invited to join that very Protestant phenomenon, the world-famous Glasgow Orpheus Choir. Under its formidable conductor, Sir Hugh Roberton, it had been going since 1901, when believe it or not, this very proper assembly had begun as a Working Men's Club. The choir *was* Hugh Roberton – or HSR, as he was known. The choir grew up around him, and when he retired fifty years later, the choir did too. It was later resurrected as the Phoenix Choir, but the magnificence of the Orpheus could never be replicated.

Roberton had fused this very respectable collection of schoolteachers and genteel typists into a unique vocal blend. They were dedicated to their collective sound, which was the very antithesis of Glasgow singing as the common man knew it. This was the sound that angels might have made had they lived in Kirkintilloch or Milngavie. Their sound, in their hymns and Scottish psalms, was as sanctified as any *Te Deum* sung in the Sistine Chapel. Although I'm certain that whether in kirk or chapel, under the stars or by the light of day, all such sounds reach Heaven.

Coincidentally, my finest memory of Glasgow singing was in a church. It was during the sixties, while I was working on *This Man Craig* for BBC Television at Queen Margaret Drive, and one Sunday morning I was a member of a packed congregation at St Aloysius Jesuit Church in Garnethill. The hymn being sung (in English) was 'How Great Thou Art' and after only a couple of lines, I was aware, as was everyone around me, that a wonderful female voice was with us that morning. At the second verse, I just couldn't help myself, I had to turn round and see the source of that smooth, languid sound. And there was 'Simone Signoret' in a belted trench coat, fair hair hanging down from a black beret that almost covered her face, but not the wonderful sound that came from her lips.

With her hands in her pockets, she stood leaning against a pillar, haloed in the morning sunlight and singing like an angel. It was ethereal, and the congregation, recognising this, went willingly mute so that 'Simone' might be heard. I have no idea who this young woman was. With those looks and that voice, she ought to have been a star. Maybe she was and I just didn't recognise her, but whoever she was, she created an unforgettable moment for everyone there.

That's what good, easy, seemingly effortless singing can do. And every Glasgow singer, whatever the occasion, considers that he or she is in that class. Would that they were. However, one Glasgow singer who would not wish to be involved in this rarefied group – indeed, he would have been appalled at the very idea of being thought holy – was Glasgow's own singer of the streets, the already-mentioned late, great Matt McGinn.

Wee Matt was that rarer article, a folk singer who couldn't really sing, yet he was a true poet who touched every vernacular song he wrote with the brush of genius. Calton born and bred, he had a flirtation with Oxford as a student at Ruskin College, and intended being a teacher. Songs, however, kept coming out of him to such an extent that he fled the classroom for the school playground and found his first audience 'among the weans'. He wrote his songs in their street language and told his stories as children would tell their own stories to each other. 'The Red Yo-yo' now has the status of a nursery rhyme with Glasgow children. McGinn wasted no time trying to please with literary effects or fine-blown poesy. He used his words as bricks and he built his songs until they were as solid as the tenement he knew so well. And when a brick wouldn't fit, he threw it at the nearest pompous target.

For a wee man, he had a big heart and an even bigger brain but he tried to hide that. He well knew the value of the Glasgow saying, 'Kid oan yer daft an' ye'll get a hurl fur nothin'. Matt laboured hard at his working-man's lyrics but you'd never guess from the ease with which they trip off the tongue. He was no singer, but his gruff, throaty sound was just right for the cheeky stuff he wrote. He got laughs aplenty when working the folk clubs with his regular guitarist, Billy Davidson, but he could also produce an unexpected lump in the throat, without being sentimental. He knew exactly what Robert Wilson meant by the right way being the hard way. But that was his way, often to the annoyance of family and friends, and to the astonishment of strangers, who couldn't believe the pugnacity and energy that this little fellow in the cloth cap exuded from the folk club dais. He was all Glasgow, and Glasgow loved him for it – after he'd gone.

I toured with him several times and he exasperated me beyond belief but he also made me laugh, and although I knew him well, he could astonish me with a beautiful line or an unexpected couplet. I once asked him what famous song he would liked to have written. Without any hesitation, he replied, 'Bridge Over Troubled Water' by Simon and Garfunkel. Poor, dear, wee Matt – he was always trying to build his own bridges, reaching out to Mr and Mrs Glasgow and their weans in his songs. But troubled domestic waters, mostly of his own making, and a total lack of money sense dragged him down before he could get his fundamental message across: that all songs were love songs.

Matt's music primer in his younger days would have been Glennie's Song Book, which you could buy at any newsagent. It was just a few sheets of cheap paper with the words of every current popular song printed so small you needed to read it under the light of the lamp post but that's how your Glasgow singer was trained – learning them by heart and then singing them with heart. You haven't heard 'Why Did You Make Me Care?' until you've heard a Glaswegian sing it; or 'Missed the Saturday Dance', which my mother used to sing as soon as her minuscule Bacardi and Coke began to take effect. Lena Martell (otherwise known as Helen Thomson) took this kind of ballad-sing to starry heights, although she could also give value to 'The Old Rugged Cross'. Then Lulu (a McNeil from Dennistoun) blew all the ballads away in a burst of exuberant rock 'n roll. Even so, Tin Pan Alley is still down Memory Lane as far as many of us are concerned. Life has changed for all of us but the song's the same and the melody lingers on. So let's hear it for the chanter. Best of order please – one singer, one song.

CHAPTER ELEVEN

The Glasgow Greens

GREEN'S PLAYHOUSE

GEORGE GREEN WAS BORN at 83 Back Lane in Preston, Lancashire in 1861, the son of a master cabinetmaker of the same name and his wife, Susannah Green, née Richmond. The Green family was old English Catholic, part of an established Lancastrian tradition of Catholicism, centred on Stonyhurst College, which resisted the Reformation and survives to this day. Young George was educated accordingly and then apprenticed to a watchmaker. In 1879, his father came into ownership of a travelling sideshow based in Wigan as part-payment of a bad debt. Not knowing what to do with it, he gave it to his son in 1880. George abandoned his trade as a watchmaker and took to the road as a travelling showman, a road that would ultimately lead him to Glasgow.

At first he toured locally around Lancashire and Yorkshire, meeting his future wife Ann Jane Bradley (known to all as Jinnie) on a visit home to Preston. He married her in 1889 and when their first child, John, was born the following year in a van in the Prince Henry Field at Lancaster, George was described on the birth certificate as 'Proprietor of Hobby

Horses'. By 1907, George and Jinnie boasted four sons and six daughters. At that time, a large family was not uncommon as it was a measure parents took to counter the high rate of infant mortality. Numbers were one assurance of family survival.

Their burgeoning family was a tribute not only to George's potency and Jinnie's stamina but also to the confidence and resilience both epitomised as travelling people. Buoyed by their Catholic faith, as well as a healthy faith in themselves, the Greens moved steadily onwards and upwards trailing their many children behind. George marched to the beat of his own drum, and even if he listened to it intently he was always smart enough to keep one ear to the ground. He was a great believer in his own hunch about things, an instinct that was to pay off splendidly for him before long.

However, at this stage, with an ever-growing family, the Greens were in danger of running out of caravans, or wagons as they called them, but having so many children would also be to their advantage because they were to be the basis of the future labour force that would serve the family so well. As soon as each child was old enough, he or she would be set to work on some aspect of travelling show business, although George made sure that the boys were sent to good Catholic boarding schools like Dowanside, Stonyhurst and St Joseph's, Dumfries. The girls were educated whenever and wherever the caravans halted.

By 1893, George Green's touring orbit included Scotland, and his annual visits to Glasgow were a summer occasion every citizen, especially in the poorer areas, looked forward to. Carnivals had been coming to Glasgow since medieval times. The various fairgrounds were almost as old as the city itself and they hadn't changed much over the centuries. They brought colour, music and amusement to the people on whose curiosity and gullibility the travelling folk relied on for a living. People were people, whether they lived in Lancashire or Lanarkshire, and these strange travellers with their tanned faces and painted caravans had all the exotic allure of gypsies to the people of the tenements, who were easily persuaded to part with their pennies and halfpennies in return for a bit of excitement. They didn't need to be enticed to come to the Fair, they came willingly. And they came in foolish numbers, for it's true (as Barnum said) that one is born every minute. 'Roll up! Roll up! A penny for the peep show!'

Green's Showground on Vinegar Hill was already becoming a mecca for travelling shows. Buffalo Bill appeared there in 1891 with his Red

Indians in a Western extravaganza and it was said that the native Americans became so enamoured with the East End pubs, particularly the old Coffin Bar in Whitevale Street, that some elected to remain in Glasgow when the Cody troupe returned to America. Reservation life, however, might not have prepared them for life on the Barrowfield housing estate but a few brave ones might have hidden up a Camlachie close, possibly communicating with each other by smoke signals from the rooftop chimneys.

An issue of *The Baillie*, a weekly Glasgow newspaper, dated 20 July 1892, gives a contemporary account of what the carnival was like for Glaswegians in Victorian times:

> 'Tis night. The flare of lamps!! The shows are open!!! M'yes – the Fair, you say. Strange place. Very oily perfume. Vinegar intervening... Switchback – very racy – ruddle uddle – hair on end – hold like mad – screams of women – Ladies, beg pardon – sort of journey. Glad you're back with your spinal column shattered. Sort of mad pleasure. When you come off you wonder if you've got feet or simply flying through the paraffin air... Hobby horses – mixture of switchback, ocean wave and merry-go-rounds. Very nice – halfpence [worth] plentiful. Ladies enjoy excitement – would go round all night and next day too. Steam whistle – also organ, very musical. No ear required, can't mistake tunes... Circuses, wild-beast shows. Surge with crowd. Another parting shot at Sally, dolls, bells and bottles...

George Green knew his audience and he was always on the lookout for new moneymaking ideas to attract them while the family was off the road in the winter. Not that the Greens were penniless. There was no taking in of pots and pans to mend or the selling of clothes pegs round the doors. They were by no means tinkers: by working hard and travelling long, they had made a good living from the 'shows' and George's adventurous attitude to life reflected this. The Greens were by now aristocrats of the road with wagons like yachts on wheels boasting opulent interiors that shone with polished rosewood and gleaming brass. He wasn't the son of a master carpenter for nothing. If fortunes were to be told by these gilded gypsies, George might well have studied his own hand, for the lines of his future success were already clearly marked. He was avid for novelty and he never stopped looking ahead.

For instance, while wintering comfortably at the showground site on Vinegar Hill at the Old Barracks off the Gallowgate at Camlachie – and also while awaiting the birth of Winifred, the first of his daughters to be born in Glasgow – he toyed with the idea of manufacturing mineral waters. When Veronica, daughter number three, was born at the Old Barracks in 1893, her birth certificate still described her father as a 'Mineral Water Manufacturer'. Although he continued to make the product on the campsite George found that soft drinks didn't bring in sufficient hard cash. Typically, he began to look around for something else to do with himself in the Glasgow winter. At the time, the new fad from the United States was Mr Edison's kinematograph for the showing of pictures that *moved*. This aroused Green's always-alert, entrepreneurial instincts, and, true to form, he took immediate action and bought a train ticket to London. He went there to find out for himself more about this new toy from Edison's British counterpart, William Friese-Green, who traded as Friese-Green and Paul. George met with Friese-Green, and, as a result, came away with one of the first projectors made in Britain for the showing of film.

Returning to his East End showground, complete with instructions, he quickly set up a screening booth in time for the Christmas season of 1896. It was quite a rudimentary affair. A white sheet was hung at one end of a tent and the projector threw a series of images on to it from the other. These images flickered constantly, but the public loved it and flocked to see the 'flickers', or 'flicks', as they came to be called. It was merely another form of peep show but George Green knew from the start he was on to a winner. Not for the last time, he had gauged public feeling and gave them what they weren't aware they wanted until he offered it to them. He built a mobile version of this kinematographic booth, measuring fifty by thirty feet, and called it his 'Theatre Unique'. It was as unique as he was. If a prophet is not without honour save in his own country, then George, as an Englishman in Scotland, was entitled to expect the honour of a profit at least.

Astutely, he added seating and upped admission prices from a penny to threepence, adding a cup of tea and a biscuit to sweeten the increase. The mobile booth took its place in the Green caravanserai as a sideshow in itself, and was drawing in more than twenty pounds a day. This was serious cash by Edwardian standards, and the Greens were 'in the money'. This was just as well, for three more daughters had been born meantime. George could now well afford such a life investment and he looked for a similar return to his 'kinema' enterprise. It was the success of the booth that gave him the idea of a permanent building for the housing of the kinematograph. He began by buying up the shells of the disused roller skating rinks that had existed around Glasgow during the skating craze only a few years before. Now that everyone was kinematograph crazy, the George family adapted the old rinks as 'kinemas'. The Green foundations in Glasgow had been laid.

At the same time, a Mr Ralph Pringle was touring around the city with his North American Animated Cinematograph (note the new spelling) and in 1907 he rented the Queen's Theatre at Glasgow Cross and, calling it Pringle's Picture Palace, (the first Three P's), opening it solely for the showing of moving pictures. This confirmed George Green's hunch about the public's appetite for film, so he sold up his fairground and circus assets in 1908 and bought the old thousand-seater Whitevale Music Hall in Dennistoun. It was this theatre, not far from the Old Barracks site, that became the Whitevale Moving Picture House. It was the Greens' first cinema proper, and continued to serve as the Whitevale until the 1970s. George's oldest son, John, a great favourite with everyone, and the apple of his father's eye, was installed as its first manager. John Green was just eighteen but had all of his father's energy and commercial nous and, choosing to live above the shop, he moved into the tenement flat in the adjacent close. With his formidable mother's help, and his sisters at hand, he got down to business. Jinnie leased out land behind the theatre as parking space for touring caravans so that a cash-flow was maintained while they built up their 'kinema'. The older girls assisted at the box office and with administration. In this way, salaries were kept to a minimum, allowing profits to be ploughed back into the firm. As far as possible, everything was kept in the family, and this became the first rule in all the Greens' further commercial dealings.

By 1911, cameras and film stock had improved sufficiently to eradicate much of the flickering so the flicks gradually became 'the movies' to the public, simply because the pictures moved. It was in this same year, in the Gorbals, that George opened the first of a chain of 'Picturedromes', the new name coined for the kinemahouses, as the

Greens still called them. With their second son, Fred, now out of school and in the business, things began to build up. Fred was a huge man and from the beginning he thought big. The Green interests expanded with him. Soon, as Green's Film Services, George had enough Picturedromes in the group to give one to each of his children, but then, in 1914, came the first big family tragedy.

John Green, of whom so much was expected, died suddenly at the age of twenty-four. The shock so affected George Green that he retired to his wagon on Vinegar Hill and within a year, he himself was dead at fifty-four. The strain of hyper-activity had eventually told, even if precipitated by the death of his son and heir. The death of both John and George was a loss to the city as much as to the family. The huge amount of letters of condolence reaching the Greens in the Gallowgate testified to the status the family had won in Glasgow society and the high standing both father and son had among their peers. The Greens were now fully accepted as Glaswegians.

Jinnie Green was now left with a very large organisation to support but with almost as big a fortune, all of which had grown from that first penny-a-head experiment in the booth which her husband had initiated and her first son had carried on. Now both were dead, but the many other Greens were still very much alive. In 1918, the matriarch and her busy brood formed themselves into a film servicing company with offices in Glasgow and London. A third brother, Bert, now came into the fold as manager, working in tandem with Fred, and soon they had branched out into making films themselves with Green's Topical Productions. They also pioneered a filmed newsreel in Scotland for showing in their cinemas and even published their own magazine, *Green's Kinema Tatler*. Thus the seeds were sown for a cinema empire that would eventually extend into Europe. The question now was whether they would outgrow Glasgow – or would film-mad Glasgow grow quickly enough as a cinema city to contain them? George Green's surviving sons, Fred and Bert, had all their father's flair and showmanship and the daughters had their mother's gift for management. Altogether, they were a formidable commercial force.

In the early twenties, Fred Green went to Hollywood as much as his father had gone to London almost thirty years previously. Fred was drawn there by the appeal of Douglas Fairbanks and his wife, Mary Pickford, who, with Charlie Chaplin as a partner, formed United Artists as an independent company aimed at breaking away from the strict studio control. This was the first declaration of star power. As was said at the time, the inmates had taken over the asylum. Perhaps so, but Fred Green was sane enough to see the commercial advantage in being involved with such a powerful triumvirate. He was frequently to be on the various film sets with Chaplin and the rest but there is no record of his ever going in front of the camera. It would have needed cinemascope to contain the larger-than-life Fred. His love affair with Hollywood was immediate and lasting. The stars were kind to him because they knew they were wooing an investor, but Fred also knew he was making a valuable investment. The Greens were in the big time and ready to go even bigger.

Fred came back full of American ideas for his cinema group and, at the same time, keen to upgrade his status on the private front. The family began to invest in domestic property and bought up a series of stately mansions in Dumbreck, near Bellahouston Park. If they were moving out of their wagons, they wanted to make sure that the fixed, stone-built alternatives were just as comfortable. Every admission ticket sold at the Greens' cinemas was another brick cemented into the family's property portfolio. Fred and his English wife, 'Bunchy' Paterson, moved into Craigie Hall, a veritable mini-estate on Rowan Road, complete with tennis courts, croquet lawns, and staff to match. There were American cars in the garage (former stables), complete with live-in chauffeur. Fred and his wife had style. They entertained appropriately and lavishly. Having no children they adopted all their Glasgow friends.

From the 'mother-hen' mansion that was Craigie Hall, all the other Green chickens came to roost in what amounted to a Green enclave within a corner-kick of Ibrox Stadium. Bert and his wife Marjorie bought 'Glen Ard' on the corner of Rowan Road and Beech Avenue, while Margaret and her husband bought 'Ashcroft' on the opposite corner. Marion, the youngest sister, was given 'Belltrees' on Maple Road, a house she would later pass on to her sister, Nona, and her husband, Celtic footballer Jimmy McGrory, as a wedding present. It could be said that all the Green family were now accepted as part of the Glasgow bourgeoisie. Their caravans had finally come to rest.

Meantime, Fred and Bert were supervising the building of a super entertainment centre in the heart of the city. This was to become the famous Green's Playhouse at the top of Renfield Street and the largest cinema in Europe. It even featured a hall above the cinema to cater for the latest current craze – ballroom dancing. Fred and Bert were determined to bring their own kind of Hollywood to Glasgow and they embarked on a building project that would give the city a landmark that would be known and loved by Glaswegians for generations. Everything in the new Playhouse was to be the biggest and the best, and by careful planning and judicious use of their own workforce, they were to achieve these aims with style. Bruce Peter in his *100 Years of Glasgow's Amazing Cinemas*, explained how they did this:

> The brothers were astute businessmen. Whenever possible they used the Greens' own employees to do the building work. Clowns, acrobats and showmen, usually employed elsewhere in the company, were taught plumbing, joinery and bricklaying and set to work. The scheme was so carefully budgeted that, to save on travel costs, the workers walked every day from Green's Gallowgate showground to the Renfield Street site...

No expense was spared in planning this super-cinema. Red and golden luxury double seats, known as 'divans' were installed in the balcony for courting couples interested in things other than the film. To the Glaswegians, the divans quickly became the 'dive-ons' and well-used by young couples. Who knows how many dived into matrimony from the heady heights of the Playhouse circle? In the other levels, 4,368 plush seats were available and the dance floor above them could accommodate 6,000 dancers. The Greens gambled on the dance craze becoming as big as the film craze, and once again they were right. Football, dancing and film-going formed the great trinity of Glasgow passions.

The Playhouse cinema, theatre and ballroom complex was opened with great ceremony on Thursday 15 September 1927 by Mrs David Mason, wife of the Lord Provost of Glasgow, in the presence of all the local dignitaries and personalities from the sporting world, as the Green brothers were known to be interested in football and boxing. In every way, these English Greens, fairground folk as they were, completely mirrored the vitality and dynamism of the teeming city which had adopted them. They were admired for their industry and drive and for the genius the family had for taking pains. No more so than in the Playhouse project where nothing had been left to chance.

A full orchestra under Gordon Ritchie accompanied the silent films and a troupe of dancers featured in the stage shows. The visual impact of the rich interior was magical in its effect. The Greens had obviously not forgotten their carnival roots. First impressions counted with the public. Curiosity is the first stage of commitment. Get people to come through the doors and you can then persuade them to put their hands in their pocket. The Greens knew this and planned their interior accordingly. The main staircase was marble, pillars adorned the restaurant and theatrical balustrades decorated the foyer. The whole interior was ablaze in orange, primrose and gold, and rich carpet was everywhere. This was a film house which itself looked like a Hollywood set. Zigzag neon strips in the ceiling gave the effect of lightning and added to the dramatic impact on patrons. The Greens had never attempted anything on this scale before, and the result made Glasgow gasp.

George Singleton, himself a noted Glasgow cinema proprietor and owner of the famous Cosmo on Rose Street (now the Glasgow Film Theatre), was to write of the Greens:

> For private individuals to invest so heavily in such a marvellous project, way before the advent of talkies, must have taken great courage indeed. I always admired the Greens for their boldness; their Glasgow Playhouse was a most remarkable theatre.

You couldn't miss it. A huge electric sign told all of Glasgow that the brand new 'GREEN'S PLAYHOUSE' was now in business and showing Monte Ray in *Play Safe* as the main attraction.

Going uptown to the Playhouse was to become a Glasgow experience, one way or another, for the next half-century. It was a showplace for millions of Glaswegians who passed through its portals to sit in the dark or dance in the spotlight. Whatever you chose to watch, it was an experience few people forgot. Watching a film is as much an emotional event as dancing a slow foxtrot or tango, and it is just as subjective. You can lose yourself in a film and sometimes you're reluctant to rise up and go out again into the street to face that other world which doesn't seem nearly as real as the one you've just left.

Movie madness brought with it Art Deco and this became the design base for most of the cinemas that flooded Glasgow following the building of the Playhouse. At La Scala on Sauchiehall Street you could have a meal while watching a film although it was hard to think of watching Myrna Loy while eating steak and chips. The foresight shown by the Greens at their Playhouse is underlined by the current fashion in big cities of cinemas now offering screenings complete with dinner menu and bar service while you watch. Modern cinemas call this kind of film-going Gold Service Cinema, but no one, however, has come up with the inviting 'dive-on'.

I can see now that certain cinemas stand as staging posts through my stumbling youth. They were stations of the cross I had to bear for being brought up among the tenements. My boyhood was left in the Black Cat. My youth began at the Granada and I came of age at the Cosmo. Going to the pictures was a continuing phase of our general education. For those who did not aspire to a tertiary education, and indeed were lucky to survive primary, the local picture house offered a whole range of tuition in history, biography, music and world literature, and all for the price of admission.

I was convinced that Don Ameche invented the telephone at the Three P's (the Parkhead Picture Palace) on Tollcross Road. It was Tyrone Power who built the Suez Canal, and Paul Muni discovered the antiseptic value of carbolic soap. It was only later I read about Alexander Graham Bell, de Lessops and Pasteur. Similarly, the music of Chopin was introduced to us by Cornel Wilde, the life and work of Rembrandt by Charles Laughton, and as far as we were concerned, Basil Rathbone *was* Sherlock Holmes. This was film as night school with a black and white screen instead of a blackboard, cheesecake for chalk, and a glamorous leading lady instead of a baldy teacher with a speech impediment. How could we resist it?

Glasgow, however, had a total antipathy to what were called *English* pictures. As soon as the Gainsborough lady appeared, nodding her white-wigged head there were loud jeers. The Mayfair accents provoked loud laughter and the horsey heroines were scoffed at. It was a very different matter, however, with French or Italian films, and that's where the Cosmo came in. It was a small, privately-owned picture house on Rose Street, off Sauchiehall Street, and for the Glasgow youth who aimed to be worldly, this was their venue for instruction. Most adolescent boys in Glasgow were introduced to the female breast within its dimly-lit walls, or at least to the delectability of the cleavage. I'm not sure girls got the same thrill from the leading man's moustache but I know that it was the Cosmo which introduced young Glaswegians to sin as an art form.

It was no accident that so many picture houses were called 'Palaces'. Taking their lead from the Greens, cinema-owners turned their premises into magnificent piles, thickly-carpeted and sweetly-scented, tastefully-lit, and, most of all, with seats like armchairs, just made for dreaming. It was all a fantasy world and it drew people from the streets like the veritable Mecca each cinema was. It was as much a part of a Glasgow childhood as the weekly comic. These are memories etched in celluloid and they never fade or corrode. We can still run the reels through our mind's eye and re-live the magic moments all over again. All cinemas, from the biggest Palace to the smallest flea-pit, look the same in the dark and watching faces show silvered in the glow from the screen, are rapt, lost in the living cinema moment.

George Green could have had no idea what he started in Glasgow. Fred Green could never have foreseen that the Playhouse, after an uneasy spell as a rock and roll venue until 1972, would be allowed to fall derelict and be pulled down only weeks before it was to be awarded status as a listed building. Bert would have remembered that nearly half a million people passed through its impressive portals to see Larry Parks in *The Jolsen Story* when that 'wonder film', as it was called, ran for three weeks in February 1947. Ah, those were the days.

But new days are coming. There is now a virtual Cinema City in Govan. The film people are lovin' Govan and, who knows, great things may yet come out of their new workshops as were ever created in the shipyards they have replaced. Artists are once again united and, given time, we could uncover our own Chaplin. Edinburgh may have had its *Trainspotting* but Glasgow could score with its 'trend-spotting'. Forsyth Hardy may have been a force in the infant Scottish film world but Bill Forsyth's *Gregory's Girl* caught the international eye and others, such as Peter Mullen, have held its attention ever since.

Ken Loach came to Glasgow to make *Ae Fond Kiss* and confirmed that the city is now a place to make movies, where once we merely watched them. The former Cinema City was a thing of buildings but now it is the centre of modern film ideas, as recent films like *Wilbur Wants to Kill Himself* and *Sweet Sixteen* have shown. International actors like Robert Carlyle even live in the city now and others, such as Billy Connolly, Lulu, Gregor Fisher, Dorothy Paul, Bill Paterson and so many more, are just waiting for someone to call 'Action' in their native city. It could be the start of something big: something on the Green scale.

Scottish Screen Services in Glasgow exists to help Scottish filmmakers reach out to the world. For instance, the Argentinian writer Alberto Manguel, mentioned in the Preface of this book, plans to film his Stevenson-based novel in Govan. The G-force not only applies to Glasgow but also to the phenomenon of the new Gollywood in Govan. G is also for George. Film Glasgow owes much to George Green and his family and, thanks to them, the dear green places were suddenly upholstered and transformed into dear, Green playhouses at all points of the city. By George, it was quite an undertaking, but Glasgow had its own word for it: it was *magic*.

CHAPTER TWELVE

No Room at The Inn on the Green

MR PIANO MAN

IN GLASGOW THE LIVING is easy. It's only a matter of breathing in and out. How long you live, however, is another matter. But whether it's Glasgow or Grimethorpe, the fundamentals of existence still apply:

> *We are born, we learn, we earn and we buy;*
> *We eat and we drink, we sleep and we die.*

Everything else outside that little couplet is a luxury, an inessential, if you were to be really honest with yourself. Attending such things you would move inexorably from the cradle to the grave, but would such a sterile application to mere survival really be called living? I don't think so. *There are more things in heaven and earth...* Things like spirit and imagination and humour and desire. There are pictures to paint, songs to sing, thoughts to have, mountains to climb, rivers to cross, even books to write, but most of all, there are people to love. Love, or the lack of it, is at the root of all things.

Love, not sex, is the source of the drive that energises us. Sex can tire you out.

> *The longer you live, the more you find*
> *You live less in the body and more in the mind.*

It takes time to realise this, but the secret is to make time to find love, to recognise it if you're lucky and live by it if you can. Time isn't life, it's only a commodity. Man invented time, or rather the artificial measurement of it, and now he has to live by it. Our ancestors lived by the season, by the movement of the sun and the moon and the tides. These were their clocks and calendars. Nowadays we have the mobile phone. Yet even in this sophisticated 'Information Age' how can you measure a 'moment'? That's the real measure of a life – the moment. And how many you can fit in from waking to sleeping? Whatever you do, however you live, and wherever you live, even in dear old Glasgow, there are moments to be made along the way; but you need to be on the look out for them at all times. As Burns so neatly put it:

> *Catch the moments as they fly*
> *And use them as ye ought, man.*
> *Believe me, happiness is shy*
> *And comes not ay when sought man.*

Oscar Wilde said it in another way when he warned us to be careful what we pray for, as our prayers might be answered. You need to know your own agenda. All of us are driven principally by material ambition – that's the way the world is. Aesthetic satisfaction is not a priority. It trails along as best it can in the economic slipstream trying to make its still, small voice heard above the market din. It is never completely silenced, however. Accountants can get excited about a row of figures in a financial statement and become quite emotional about striking a balance. However cerebral the actuary, there's a heart unaccounted for in the ledger.

I daresay the whole thing is a matter of balance, trying to level the see-saw, sorting out the demands of the left brain and the right brain and trusting in what is called, less scientifically, your 'gut feeling'. At least when you follow that, you can't blame anyone else. That's the very first step in survival; finding someone to blame. Whole careers have been founded on that principle. Come to think of it, why should we call any diligent application to a particular course of action in life, a *career*? The word itself originally referred to a racecourse and indicates a wild, headlong gallop. Hardly the way one would consider a steady lifetime advancement through a profession. It also implies a degree of care, which I suppose would be necessary in any headlong gallop. The final criterion might be that anything in life is worthwhile if your heart's in it. That's life.

> *It's obvious to me, and I understand why,*
> *You've really got to live before you can die.*

Then there is the place of the dream – the haunting image that arrives with your awakening and stays with you all day. Sometimes, a dream will remain with you all your life. It is the end aim, the final goal, the ultimate solution, but there is nothing material about it. It merely exists as a phantom, paralleling the reality we see all around us. But is never a part of it. It is the 'other' part of all of us, hovering around us, tantalisingly close but always just out of reach. It's there to nudge us now and again, to remind us that none of us is perfect and we mustn't try to be our own Gods – however worthy we think we are to aspire to that status. We are made, they say, in His image, but a family resemblance doesn't make us equals. We are merely mortal and our basic function is to go on breathing for as long as we can. And we are back where we started – breathing in and out.

These thoughts were prompted by the news that The Inn on the Green in Bridgeton was for sale. This was a venue I knew very well in its hey-day and I also knew that the place was the result of one man's fulfilling his dream, of finding a career where his heart lay, of having his prayers answered. Best of all, it gave him the opportunity of making a few moments, not only for himself but for many others in the course of his proprietorship. Now it is no more, at least as he knew it. There is no longer room at the Inn on the Green.

The Green in question is Glasgow Green, that vast rural sweep in the industrial heartland of the city that is almost a kingdom on its own. Its green suzerainty is undisputed and it lies by the northern bank of the Clyde like a Dowager Duchess about to take the waters. Its north-eastern borders touch on the highly-ornate business centre that was the former

Templeton Carpet Factory and nearby is an old tenement in front of Dunn's Lemonade Factory. It was in the cellar basement of this tenement that our story began in 1983.

Philip Raskin was, and still is, a good Glasgow Jewish boy whose father was in the rag trade. When he died suddenly, a whim of accounting left Philip in sole possession of a group of shop window mannequins stored in a basement in Bridgeton. Somehow or other, this asset had been missed in the final inventory and young Philip didn't take long to realise that this was virtually all he had in the world. At that time, he was a promising piano-playing student at the Glasgow School of Art and had vague notions of a career as an artist. Instead, he was abruptly given a crash course in the art of survival.

The underground premises he had inherited between the Carpet Factory and the Lemonade Works did not have a good address or an imposing entrance, but it had tiny windows which just about afforded a glimpse of Glasgow Green across the road. It was free from damp and had running water – so Philip decided to turn it into a restaurant. He discovered that he had an innate love for stainless steel and it was this which inspired him to create a modern kitchen out of one of the rooms off the main area. His much older affair with the piano was confirmed by the arrival of a baby grand which was given prime place in the emerging dining room under the street windows. Gradually, an attractive little restaurant grew up around it, and on 7 June 1984, The Inn on the Green, as he called it, was formally opened to the public.

Sitting back on the piano stool, Philip saw that it was good. Between chords he was his own one-man-band, making music from the rattle of plates and the clink of glasses. Slowly, with the help of his friends, his below-stairs bistro evolved to match his optimistic, and quite unrealistic, vision – to bring West End flash to East End panache. He had sunk all his hopes in cutlery and tablecloths and trusted in his Glasgow instinct which told him that if nothing was possible, it wasn't impossible either. The punters, as he called his patrons, were intrigued. They had not expected a Ronnie Scott Club tinted by a touch of Manhattan – with just enough of the old Metropole in the atmosphere to keep it from getting above itself – to rise out of a subterranean property leftover. Yet here it was, and less than a hundred yards from Brig'ton Cross.

It was Left Bank but on the right side of the park and with just enough flair to make up for the lack of floor space. Customers could come here and imagine that the Seine rather than the Clyde was on the other side of the football pitches. After listening to some good piano music, supping some delicious food and sipping some smooth wine, they could make their way home feeling they had just had a continental break. And if they could afford it, they could add a painting to their bill.

And most of them could. These were the East End brash with the West End cash. It was Mercs and Jags that were vandalised on the street outside. Few patrons came here by bus. The cigar smoke inside was expensive as well as pervasive but it all made for an atmosphere that had the slightest frisson of danger about it (and I don't mean passive smoking). The Inn on the Green would have made a perfect Chicago speakeasy had it had a little less taste, but there was no doubt the setting was individual. Mr Raskin saw to that. It always helps the mystique of any location if you have to reach it by going downstairs. You always build a stairway to Paradise going up but you had to come down to Philip's level to meet the Devil. Anyway, isn't it always said that we fall into sin? This is not to suggest for a moment that The Inn on the Green was in any way disreputable. It was very much a house of repute, but there was no denying it had an atmosphere and Glasgow people loved it – especially the men. At times, the clientele was like a men's club – for those who didn't wear ties yet had expensive suits, and others who hadn't shaved but wore watches that told everyone that their owners were having the time of their lives.

Little by little, word got round that Philip's dream was *the* place and, gradually it began to build up around him. Thanks mainly to the nearby Templeton Business Centre, a lunchtime trade developed, drawn by a witty menu and a caustic maître. Proprietor Raskin developed his own style with customers, which was a deadpan, self-deprecating, cynically decrying manner that dared them to order what he advised them against. It was an unorthodox selling tactic but then Philip was not your orthodox Jew – at least he never wore his religion on his sleeve. Whatever the reason, the gamble paid off and before long he was on first-name terms with his well-heeled regulars who obviously enjoyed his patter.

A customer here was not a patron but a partner in a double act who was cunningly made to feel that *he* was the comedian. It was a barrow-boy ploy served up in a Jaguar manner and it took the trick. As well as being a place to be seen in, The Inn on the Green became a place to see, and as a result the Raskins prospered. The fact that the blonde Mrs Barbara Raskin was beautiful, witty and highly efficient also did the business no harm. Music was still at the heart of it all and cabaret became a feature. Stars like Jimmy Logan and Marian Montgomery were to appear there in due course. However, it was the annual Burns Supper in late January – which some called the Rabbi Burns Night – that helped establish it as an entertainment centre and this is where I come in.

Just after the restaurant opened, Alannah and I had been taken to lunch there by Elspeth King, the then Curator of the People's Palace Museum just along the road in the Green. We were there to talk about performing one of our shows in the museum. There weren't many customers that day so Philip had time to talk to us, and in the course of the lunchtime chat, he asked if I'd like to 'do my Burns' in the restaurant. Looking around, I wasn't sure there was space in what looked to me like the ward-room of a submarine, and told him so. Philip was quite unperturbed and reassured me that there was no danger of depth charges. 'I charge enough as it is,' he quipped. The upshot was that I agreed to come for a trial night in the following January. 'What's the fee?' I asked before we left. 'You surely don't expect to be paid as well as fed?' replied Philip. 'Look upon it as experience.'

An experience it certainly was. I ended up playing my solo Burns show four nights from Sunday to Thursday, and went through as many dress shirts, because of the sweat running down my back under the dinner jacket. But it was a good sweat because they were great nights in every respect – a packed audience, perfect ambience, and a wonderful Burns script with which to work. Despite the presence of the redoubtable Bridgeton Burns Club in the area, these evenings created an ideal Burns atmosphere – warm, intimate, unpretentious and completely spontaneous.

There were no formal speeches or empty ritual, just an actor talking to his audience and becoming as one with them. This was not your usual matron and maiden theatre audience, but a sterner-seeming house with more men than usual, accompanied by their grown-up sons. I was amazed how many sons brought their fathers. It was these sons, and their wives, sisters and daughters, who bought out the season year after year and brought a rare smile to Philip's professional face. The evenings mixed intimacy with gaiety and in a style that could only have been Glasgow – unselfconscious enjoyment shot through with a deep sentimentality. Even after many years since those wonderland winter evenings, I can still remember the special atmosphere created by the poetry of the spoken word The end section caused the kind of silence you could have walked on. Yet, earlier, 'Tam o' Shanter' had raised the same audience to a pitch of laughter that had shaken the candles on the table.

It might have been the very success of The Inn on the Green that laid the seeds of its inevitable decline. There was a natural need to grow and expand, and Philip lifted up his eyes to the roof. He joined the big money to build a hotel out of the tenement above his premises. By a miracle of design and planning he carried the atmosphere from beneath up into the new extension and he made it just as personal and individual as his restaurant. Unfortunately, the better he made it look, the more it cost, until, in the way of big money, the purse-strings were used to slowly strangle the initiative of the artist-owner and his great dream of a hotel with a difference gradually dissipated itself among the deep-pile carpeting and luxurious mod cons.

He had lovingly worked to give the place his own idiosyncratic stamp, part art and part impudence, making it an East End landmark, but alas, for reasons that do not concern us here, it is no more as we remember it. Ironically, Philip retired to his easel where he was when it all began for him nearly twenty years before and he now lives happily ever after as a selling painter. However, the good that he made of The Inn on the Green lives on and is still 'interred in the brain'. There was at one time a little East End corner where many good memories were included in the menu. As any of his old regulars might have said:

> The boy Philip done great, so he did. The Inn on the Green, aye. Smashin' nights they were, so they were, the atmosphere an' that.

If Philip Raskin's story was a solo on the Klezmer clarinet, Tony Matteo's is a boisterous Italian *opera buffa*, featuring all the family in principal roles. The Matteos weren't as many as the Greens but they were noisier. I first heard them in a very unostentatious café at Parkhead Cross, which was run by the father and mother. Like all trading families, Jewish or Italian, Indian or Chinese, the children were in the business as soon as they were able to see over the counter. So Tony, who was to become the thriving City Merchant, started young, as did his younger brother and sister, Roberto and Linda.

There were many Italians in Parkhead and each family made its presence felt via the chain of bright little cafés that garlanded the district. These cafés were as well spaced as the pubs. There was virtually one in every other building in every main street. You could walk around Glasgow going from 'Tallies' to 'Tallies' and never have a wafer out of your mouth. If you were up to it, you could do the same with a chip, for there were just as many chip shops. Indeed, the contribution of the Italians to Glasgow nutrition – and to the high incidence of tooth decay – was formidable

In the First World War, Italy was on our side but Mussolini backed the wrong horse in the Second World War and the poor Glasgow Italians were the losers. Many Parkhead families lost their fathers to various prisoner-of-war camps set up around Scotland in the ludicrous notion that these amiable tradesmen were aliens or enemy agents. If we couldn't understand some of them, the Germans certainly wouldn't. Never mind, these wartime innocents were herded into trains and buses and whisked off to unknown destinations, despite the tears of their wives and the protests of their customers. Some even went overseas – to Rothesay or the Isle of Man.

The Glasgow people bore them no animosity whatsoever, and many were just sorry that sugar rationing affected the quality of their ice cream wafers. Everyone was glad to see them back at the end of the war, if only to resume the social occasion the Tallies offered each night to Glasgow youths with no money and too much time to kill. A whip-round would always yield enough to invest in a couple of McCallums, a thin coffee and a dish of pea-brae. Shared among at least half a dozen of us it gave us a night among the lights with a look at the girls and access to the jukebox. No expensive club gave more pleasure even though the proprietor might justifiably grumble about such small expenditure taking up so much of his commercial real estate. But those padded seats were so comfortable, and the chat was great. Glaswegians have had a love affair with Italian cafés ever since.

It must be said that two thirds of the Matteo attraction was the young sister, the exotic Linda, who spoke Italian and Glaswegian with equal fluency, and used both to keep her many admirers at bay. She was the siren who lured patrons daily to La Bon Appetit, as the little café was called. At the time, Linda was at least eighteen. When the Post Office next door became available, the Matteo family bought it and opened it in due course as the Duke of Touraine restaurant and bar. 'The Duke' was one of the titles of the Duke of Hamilton, the local landowner, hence Duke Street. The old Post Office had been a Parkhead institution, and now the Matteo brothers and sister were to make the same out of the Duke of Touraine.

With Roberto in the kitchen, Linda on the drinks and Tony out front as the genial host taking orders, the young triumvirate was an immediate success with the customers. Tony also invited me to perform the solo Burns Supper for his customers. One year I did so, but I was more than an hour late in getting to the restaurant as I had to fly in from Moscow. This didn't please one East End lady who said I should have got a taxi. She prefixed 'taxi' by an adjective I needn't mention, but then she did come from Carntyne (so Tony told me).

Although there were many successful Suppers at The Duke over the years, and before some distinguished audiences, most of them high-ranking police officers; it was the solo McGonagall that packed them in at Parkhead Cross. McGonagall was a costume show, but not having a dressing room on the premises, I used the kitchen to change into his Victoriana. At first I changed in the gents, but being found there once by one of those same high-ranking policemen with my trousers down, it was thought that decency would be better served if I changed among the whirling waiters and hot plates. Over the years, I even took to getting into McGonagall clothes in my mother's flat in Dennistoun and driving to Parkhead Cross, despite her misgivings.

'Ye cannae go oot intae the street like that.'

I told her not to worry, nobody would notice. And they didn't. People had seen everything in that street. One old guy in big boots, striped pants, frock coat and a big black hat with a shawl around his shoulders didn't bother them.

One night, I even walked to the restaurant dressed for the part, as it was less than half an hour from door to door. As I shambled along the pavement, one lady offered me a coin from her purse. I waved it away politely. 'Ye look that fit-sair,' she said. It was the big boots that did it. But that's Glasgow folk for you. They'll always spot someone worse off than themselves, and their first instinct is to 'gie them a wee haun', as they say.

The Matteos certainly didn't need 'a wee haun'. For them, business boomed and they moved premises upward and onward to Ingram Street.

But, as with The Inn on the Green, attempts at expansion spoiled the very special quality that the The Duke had in Parkhead. Customers can detect this very subtle change, as can performers. It's something in the ambience, the combination of place and personnel that is exactly right and matching, which doesn't seem to work when transplanted. This is what makes catering to the public a very delicate business for all those involved. Time imposes its own changes. In any case, Linda married, Roberto took up golf and Tony escaped for a time to Upper Perthshire, before returning to Glasgow to open the hugely successful City Merchant restaurant in Candleriggs. Tony had come a long way from Parkhead Cross but all the Matteos have done their parents proud, and attained their dreams for them. They had also given their patrons some memorable nights in their various establishments over the years, and made some good friends – especially, as mentioned, the high-ranking policemen – but as another Italian, Durante Alighieri, better known as Dante, might have said, 'la comedia est finito'.

Not quite, for the Irish in Glasgow had to make their mark too. They had to realise their own dream after the nightmare of the Great Famine. The Irish didn't go into the restaurant business, however – they took over pubs. No clarinet or operatic flourish here, it was more of an Irish jig. To be honest, it was less of a jig and more a case of a reel from door to door. There were sixty-six pubs between Parkhead Cross and Glasgow Cross, and Dan Flynn owned two of them, the 'Old Straw House' at the Cross in Parkhead and the Springfield Vaults, otherwise known as Flynn's at Springfield Toll. This was my father's local, just because it was the nearest to us in Williamson Street. I remember Friday nights: I had to go in and tug at his trousers to tell him to come home. Sometimes, I pulled at the wrong trousers and got a back-heel in exchange. I learned to side step quickly. The men weren't too serious, though – their own sons would be in for them soon and for the same reason.

Flynn's was called the 'funeral shop' because the funeral cars always stopped there for a drink on their way to or from Dalbeth, the Catholic cemetery just along the London Road. Dan Flynn's son, Tom, who was a bit older than I was, served behind the bar. I remember his bright red hair, blonde eyelashes and blue eyes. It was a very Irish look. My little Grannie Cairney in Baillieston was Irish – she had red hair too, but I never noticed her eyelashes. Eyelashes, however, came into prominence in more recent times when the pubs gave way to clubs and barmaids took over from red-haired sons of publicans. There had been clubs before, of course, like the Piccadilly Club, the '101' and the Stage and Screen Club, giving a nod towards sophisticated drinking in sophisticated places. However, it was not until the Year of Culture in 1990 that Glasgow got the confirmation that she could move upmarket with some justification. The Glasgow gourmet was discovered and, suddenly, eating out was 'in'.

The Ubiquitous Chip was Glasgow's restaurant of the year in 1984 and hasn't looked back since, despite crossing Byres Road from its original site. The Curlers nearby is still going strong, though the only ice you'll see there will be in your drink. The Rogano made the move from posh pub to restaurant with ease, but the Gay Gordon could hardly live up to its name, could it? Ye Old Scotia Inn on Stockwell Street is an ancient hostelry but thrives today as the folk singer's mecca. It has occupied that site since 1834, which makes it older than most of the folk songs. However, even older is the Kirk House on Shettleston Road. In the late eighteenth century it served the graveyard next door, but there is no record of dead men walking. The Doublet on Park Road was my student pub in the fifties and it hasn't changed a bit – except for the barmaid, perhaps. It was always crowded but at least it made it cosy and was as good a place as any to spend your grant. The Alpha on St Vincent Street attracted the younger patron mainly because of its pop music. Like The Inn on the Green, it is below ground level but they say it keeps the noise down. The Clarendon on Maryhill Road is for the jazz fan and Peter Keenan's boxing bar is strictly for the sportsman. Half pints of shandy do not go down well in either place.

So it's 'Time, ladies and gentlemen, please' for this Glasgow through the drinking glass. Still, I hope you can see that Glasgow caters for every taste, but, a warning: keep an eye on every church you pass. It's most likely to be the latest trendy place and a good curry is as likely to be on the menu as chop suey or a Pad Thai, but I can tell you they won't be serving altar wine or holy water. I am also certain that Philip, Tony and Tom, and all the other chasers of dreams I have known, would do the same again if they had they had to start all over. I know I would myself.

> If I had my life to live over,
> I'd live it,
> Not give it
> Up to safety

And the sensible way.
I'd make more mistakes,
Take more chances,
Make sure my troubles were real
And not imagined.
They would then be worth the bother,
If I had my life to live over.

If I had my life to live over,
I'd try for more 'moments',
As many as I could.
And I would
In every fresh day
Cherish the new,
Instead of always having to explain the old.

I would be bold,
Never dread what lay ahead,
But take it as it comes,
Good or bad – and be glad.
I would sing more loudly,
Dance more abandonedly,
Love less guiltily,
Sleep more soundly,
Waken optimistically.

If I had my life to live over,
I would live it,
Right up to the last gasp,
Which would not be a sigh,
But a 'Hallelujah!'

CHAPTER THIRTEEN

Nostalgia for a Tenement

NIGHT MUSIC

I TOOK MY FIRST steps out into the world from a tenement close in Parkhead and, to be frank, whatever direction I took would not have been backward. My street was the kind of place you left from; you didn't go there, unless you were visiting a relative or friend. Half of these people are gone now because only half the street now physically exists. I understand that the entire street is to be lost soon within a wider roadway plan for the area and frankly, it won't be missed. It adds nothing to Parkhead's status. Architecturally and culturally, Williamson Street, Glasgow E1, did little to enhance Glasgow's heritage. Nevertheless, I loved every dingy old stone of it. I didn't need to write my name on any of them because these very stones had embedded themselves in me.

My old Parkhead has virtually gone but, as I have suggested already, the name will remain in the public domain as long as Celtic FC stay in business. My building was a function, not an artefact, a utility built to accommodate as many as possible as cheaply as possible and not to last as a monument. Yet, in a sense, I was built there, so I owe it something for my first, formative years. I wasn't born there though. I was an incomer to the district, being brought in as a baby in 1931 from rural Baillieston, as it was then, when my mother and father got their first house. This was a rented room and kitchen at 20 Williamson Street near Springfield Toll, where London Road crosses Springfield Road. This was the heart of my village. From here the world as I knew it radiated – it was my patch for the first quarter-century of my life. It made me what I am, and I made it the first repository of all my hopes. Some hope, but then I didn't know any better.

I don't know why I want to write about it now, why I need to write about it at all. But if I am to write about Glasgow with any truth, I need to pin my street to the page. I know that if I conjure up my street and its once-upon-a-time way of life, I will bring it to life again for all those other Glaswegians all over the world or in that personal Glasgow they still hold in their hearts. People will call this nostalgia. So what? Nostalgia might not be what it used to be, but then neither is my old street. Never mind, the thought of it, even now, gives me a definite 'nostalgiaglasgow' – a rose-tinted glimpse of things past that maintains certain images as if they were a waxed replica of what once was. This, however, might be to do nostalgia an injustice. I consider the state to be a very necessary working aid, an armature applied to uncertain memory, a balm to the wounds that living may have inflicted on us on our way up the cliff-face. We can see then how far we have come in the life-climb and hazard a guess about how far we might have to go. If we are nearing the end, we are also nearing the peak, after which there is nowhere else to go, as far as we know, except down again. And that would be a real waste of effort, by any token. So, meantime, until we know better, we might as well hang on our ropes, wherever we are, and enjoy the view. Mine is not a pretty sight, but it is all my own, and it is from this I draw my 'Nostalgia for a Tenement':

> It's a sordid, derelict wasteland now
> Where not even weeds will grow,
> But I did, on this very spot
> Many years ago.
> For here, once stood a building,
> Proud, and clean and neat,
> Now there's no trace of that special place

In the rubble at my feet.
But I can still remember
Once upon a time...

One of my earliest images is of my wee brother, Jim, as a baby in his pram on the pavement outside the window. We were on the ground floor at the time, right at the lamp post. Its gas light was a great help and a much needed saving in gas mantles. My mother just kept the curtains open and we were lit until bedtime by courtesy of the Corporation Gas Department. During the day, babies often slept in their prams outside in the open air while their mothers got on with the housework. Jim's pram was attached to the brass well in the sink at the window by one of my father's belts. The reason for such security was not because anyone would run away with Jim, but that someone would steal the pram. My parents could easily make another baby, but they would have found it difficult in those depressing thirties to buy a new pram. Anyway, Jim says that the only thing people wanted to pinch was his little red cheeks.

What's to remember?
Please yourself:
The Family Bible on the shelf,
The jaw-box where I washed my feet
Efter tanner-baw fitbaw in the street,
Lamp posts for goalposts,
Twenty in a team
A kerb-side enclosure for letting off steam...

My sister, Agnes – named, as was the custom, after my mother's mother – arrived in due course making us what was called a 'mixed' family. We were therefore entitled to ask the factor for a bigger flat, or at least a move upstairs. This was duly achieved and we moved up to the second floor. Going up in the world had a literal meaning for tenement dwellers and soon I was looking out of the bedroom window, down on the rest of the street.

What you didn't do was look straight across at your own level as you then looked straight into other bedrooms opposite. However, even allowing for the Glasgow reluctance to close their curtains, the paper blinds were always lowered discreetly at bedtime. Sometimes, at one window, they would whirr up unexpectedly and the street was provided with a free cabaret. In which case, the light would snap off at once – which was disappointing in some cases, a relief in others. Being on the second floor also involved a stair climb several times a day, which was tough going for the oldies but no bother to a skinny wee boy.

> Up the stairs like a mountain goat
> 'O-P-E-N' from a husky throat,
> Old zinc bath ablow the bed,
> The kitchen range – shining black lead,
> The kettle never aff the boil,
> The nightly dose of castor oil,
> The squeal of pulleys through the wa'
> The woman's face that says it a'.
> Grime and grease and sentiment,
> Nostalgia for a tenement.

Sadly, it was white blinds, and not the new curtains, which closed off the street not long afterwards. My little sister died of meningitis at nine months and the shock almost killed my mother, who was only twenty-two. Something certainly died in her marriage, I think, because there were no more children for Tom and Mary Cairney. Etched in my mind ever since is the picture of my distraught father; his face unusually red, dressed in his collar and tie and best suit, coming down the stairs from our landing carrying a little white coffin under his arm, much as I had seen him carry his wooden bagpipe box when he was going off to play with the band somewhere. I don't think he saw me standing at the lower landing window. I couldn't believe that our baby sister was in that tiny white casket, and for some reason I didn't want it to touch me as it passed. I pressed myself back against the window as the solemn posse of men – my father and his two brothers, Eddie and Phil and another man I didn't know – passed on their way down to the close and out into the street to the waiting black car.

I didn't follow them. Instead I ran up to our door which was still open. My mother was sitting in my dad's chair at the fire, her eyes red from crying. The kitchen seemed to be full of women. As soon as my mother saw me, she rose up and, wiping her eyes with a hankie, said, 'Ye must be starvin'. I'll get your tea.' Then she burst out crying again –

loudly – and the women made her sit down. I was so embarrassed I didn't know what to do, but Mrs Gibson from across the landing put her arms round my shoulders and said, 'You juist come wi' me, John, an' ye kin hiv yer tea wi' ma boys.' She also had two sons. I was glad to escape.

> *Tatties an' herrin' nearly ev'ry night,*
> *Big floory scones that made yer chin a' white,*
> *Home-made soup in a cast-iron pot,*
> *Toast at the grate, the fork red-hot.*
> *Thick black treacle on soft, white bread*
> *Who can say we werena' well-fed?*

Growing up in Glasgow you learn that beauty is where you find it, and what is so wonderful about the city is that beauty can be found in the most unexpected places. But you have to keep your eyes open. Keeping your eyes skinned is not only an aid to survival in the streets, it's an assist in matters of the aesthetic as well. The same eyes will torture you with glimpses of the unsightly and the brutally ugly but you learn to live with that, too. You begin to see that even rust and dereliction can be picturesque and mildew can work wonders on any old surface. Anyway, if you live in the world of your imagination, you can see whatever you want to see. A good imagination is a crucial part of the East End survival kit.

For instance, if I stood on the seat of our outside lavatory on the lower landing and opened the little glazed window, I could look out on Stark's Joinery, and behind it, Mavor and Coulson's Wire Works, and behind that the roof of Riverside School, and behind that again the chimneys of Dalmarnock Power Station. What I saw as a boy, however, was a superimposition of all four which let me see a huge liner docked at the end of our street with its funnels, masts, and superstructure. It was always there, never put to sea, because it was only there for me. I had built it in my mind. The works, the factory, the school and the power station are all gone now – as is the little glazed window – but the ship remains in my imagination, majestically docked forever. Even though it's been there for seventy-six years, there's not a trace of rust on it. That's the benefit of mind-storage. It's free and dust-proof and it's always there when you want it.

The swan-necked well, brassy bright,
The paper blinds letting in the light,
A medal from the First World War,
Insurance money in the dresser drawer.
The knock on the brace, the wally dugs,
The hoose in the close that wis bad fur bugs,
The table cloth, for visitors only,
The man in the single-end, bachelor-lonely,
It takes all kinds to represent
Nostalgia for a tenement.

Silverdale Street was the street exactly parallel to Williamson Street going east, and no more than fifty yards to the right off London Road, but it could have been fifty miles as far as we were concerned. It was posh, you see. A better class of citizen lived in this single-sided street facing the two immaculate greens of the Belvidere Bowling Club and beyond them to the wooded grounds of Belvidere Hospital. Not many class Glasgow tenements have that kind of outlook, and if they do it's at treble the rent. Silverdale was rural in an urban situation; it looked out on to green. That must have had an effect on the people living there. We looked out our windows on to other windows that just stared back at us. Silverdale Street residents, however, looked out to grass and trees, and even if it meant gazing at the occasional backside of a bowler, you could be sure he was well-trousered. I envied these near-neighbours of ours in their neat, tiled closes facing out to the open sky. Even at the foot of their street they had the Strathclyde Juniors football ground from which the flagpole flew the Blue Saltire on match days. These days are no more but nowadays trees grow in Williamson Street and there are flower beds before the ground floor windows. The gas lamp posts have gone and tall floodlights have taken their place. With the new smoke-free regulations, the chimneys have been removed from the rooftops and the stone has been cleaned giving a lovely blush to the new face it presents. I had never known it was red – it had always looked grey to me. It's as if the street had been sick but recovered and had its healthy complexion restored. It now looks nearly as good as Silverdale Street.

Of course the other side of our street was in a U-turn from it and maybe shared the same builders. I think we got the scab Irish on our building, whose U-turn left led it into the same grey stone of Springfield

Road, but then, what was I but scab Irish myself? All the same, I still envied Silverdale Street. What both sides of the street had in common, however, was a gable end – the blank wall at the southern end – a dead end, you might say, but the metaphor was lost on us then. We took things as they were. Especially when no one was looking.

> Pipeclay patterns on the stairs,
> Sit in the sun in kitchen chairs,
> Rakin' in the midgie, beatin' carpets roon the back,
> A clean washin' hangin', the coalman's stoory sack.
> Bunker in the lobby, bed in the recess,
> The lavvy in the landing, mice in the press,
> Tea in the caddy, biscuits in the tin,
> Box in the wardrobe to keep photographs in.
> Ashes in the ash pan, wax cloth on the floor,
> You run out of sugar – just chap a neighbour's door.
> The two pound jar of rhubarb jam,
> The rattle of a late-night tram,
> Footsteps in the wet cement,
> Nostalgia for a Tenement.

As a boy, I had an instinct for better things, though God knows why. My father had the same sense of not quite belonging, but I thought all fathers were like that. He was a labourer, who was all musician. He could play the piano, the mandolin and the pipes, and he was a great singer, so I suppose he was never your ordinary working man. His constant reading told you that. He aspired to something, but he didn't aspire enough. He had that indefinable element in him called charm, which is not always a blessing. Why bother to work at a thing when a smile gets you all you want? So he fell back on the easy way out. My brother shares our father's relaxed disposition. I don't. I am my mother's son. She was fey and had the second sight but she never liked to talk about it. She didn't want to know. She preferred to concentrate on getting through the day.

> The Salvation Army's Sabbath alarm,
> The cart that came round with eggs from the farm,
> Taking your new bike out on the road,
> The Indian peddler with his heavy load.

A shilling on a Saturday, sometimes two bob,
A fortune to spend – just the job!
Sittin' in the Tallies wi' your pea-brae,
Making a McCallum last all day.
Tizer and empire biscuits – picnic in the park,
Fishing for 'baggyminnies' – home in the dark.
Nights at the carnival with some of your mates,
Long summer evenings on roller skates.
Kirby grips or a big dawd o' string,
The drawer in the sideboard had everything.
The messages you were always sent,
Nostalgia for a Tenement.

There were so many things for a boy to do in a tenement: taking down the ashes in the grate to the midden, drying the dishes on the sink-board, washing the outside of the windows (which meant standing on the concrete window sill two storeys up from ground level), carrying the carpets down to the back-court railings, where you raise the dust with a cane beater – all this had to be done in the course of a working week and there was no escaping it.

I soon became ingenious in looking for the chance to break free. This always came when my mother couldn't find her purse, prior to her daily tour of the local shops. In Parkhead, you bought for the day on the day, having little storage space in the house and none at all for perishables. Refrigeration was a matter of putting the milk, margarine and cheese in pots of cold water or in various saucers and hoping for the best on the windowsill overnight.

My mother was your typical Glasgow working-class housewife. Shy in company but never cowed, because she was essentially honest, with a brisk mind that was rarely stretched – until her old age, when she started doing the cryptic crossword in *The Herald*. She had endless energy and a capacity for love as big as Castlemilk. That didn't stop her giving me a hard time. After one terrible row, she ended up saying, 'I suppose if ye done a murder I'd still hiv tae love ye.' That's mothers for you. The only time I saw her lost for words was when she saw me play Hamlet at the Glasgow Citizens' in 1960. She was overawed by the whole play experience, something she never expected. Up to then, she had always seen 'oor John' in everything I did on stage.

One, two, three a-leerie,
See a lassie spin her peerie.
Beds on the pavement, guidies an' girds,
Skinny black cats and wee broon birds,
Step-for-a-hint – a big, white jorry,
Hudgie rides on the back of a lorry,
Jump off quick before the lights are green,
Or you end up somewhere like Aberdeen.
Leevi – moshie – cigarette cards,
The postcard from Saltcoats, 'Kind regards',
Candy-rock and dabbities, sugarolly watter.
Saving up for the school trip,
Rouken Glen or doon the watter.
The rag-man's cheeky bugle call,
Bouncing off the gable wall,
The mysterious lodger who came and went,
Nostalgia for a Tenement.

The man in the single end next to us, I can't remember his name, was a bachelor – I think. We rarely saw him, but if we ever passed on the stairs, there was always a wee smile or a nod – but never a word. I don't think he was dumb, he just never spoke out loud. But we could always see when he was in by the light under his door. We never heard his wireless or a gramophone. What did he do in that little one-room retreat? Did he talk to himself, I wonder?

If he did, Mrs Dow would have heard. She kept her ear out for everything that happened in the close. Not that she was nosy, it was just that everybody told Mrs Dow everything. She was a wonderful shoulder to lean on, or cry on. The Dows lived up our close – Number 20, one up left. Everybody knew where Mrs Dow lived. She was the unofficial street midwife and undertaker. 'She sees ye in an' she sees ye oot,' as the street put it. Her door was chapped at all hours. We could always tell whether it was an entrance or exit she had to deal with, by the laughter or the tears on the landing. Paw Dow was her amiable husband, the bunnet always on his completely bald head. Rose was the young daughter, a big, beautiful blonde girl, who went to seed just as she was beginning to flower. She added considerably to Parkhead's population, and, as they say, roasted her mother's heart. But the Dows' pride and joy was their soldier son. He had served in Palestine and he caused a sensation the first time he walked down our street in his tartan trews. He had the most glorious tan. One auld hen at her window called out, 'Hiv ye been away yer holidays, son?' Private Dow just grinned and gave her a smart salute.

Mrs Dow was respected by the whole street but there were many women like her up those nine closes in the street and the dozen families they each held. At most, there were a hundred families altogether and at one time I knew them all. There was always somebody there when you wanted them. We children knew the doors we could chap at any time and you were sure of a piece and jam or a drink of ginger till your own mother came back from the shops or the steamie. She would do the same for your pals.

> Pitch an' toss on a Sunday morning,
> Raided by the polis without any warning,
> The fly wee bookie's runner, who hings aboot the close,
> The parish boy in your class at school, who aye had a
> snottery nose.
> The girl up the next close, who married a Yank,
> The day you lost your bool down a stank.
> The clatter of screwtops on Saturday nights,
> Lining up at the broo', the rammies, the fights.
> The singsongs, the parties, the sweet smell of chips,
> Back close kisses from cold, purs'd lips,
> The Ne'er day bottle you dare not drink,
> Next morning, hungover, sick in the sink.
> Bargains at the Barras, join the menage,
> People comin' roon the doors – up to every dodge.
> The things that were stolen, the things that were leant,
> Nostalgia for a Tenement.

It was Parkhead policy to look after its own. A woman with a man idle would find a milk bottle of soup at her door or a child's cardigan hanging on the door handle. The fabric of common care was strong and not easily broken, and for those who occasionally went beyond the unwritten rule of the street, in whatever way, retribution was appropriate – and instant. Nothing was ever said but something was always done. That was the way of the street.

The rent man, the gas man,
The man with the Provy cheques,
The cruelty man, the electric man,
The School Board, the 'tecs.
Friday night at the pictures,
See you in the queue,
Standing at the corner, nothing else to do.
Spending every penny as soon as it came in,
Putting another line on, praying that you'll win.
Hard up and fed up, making both ends meet,
You get yourself in trouble and you land up in the street.
But a funeral or a wedding can always get you by
A cup of tea, a wee dram, or even steak pie.
It's all one family living on a stair,
When you have very little, you really have to share,
The accordion's two-in-the-morning lament,
Nostalgia for a Tenement.

Whatever you wanted you could always get it in the street. There was always a man who knew a man who knew a man who – whatever it was. A window pane, a new letter box, a picture frame, a cupboard to be put in or taken out, wallpapering to be scraped or hung, or house painting, it was all available – you only had to ask. This was because everyone in the street lived *on* the street. Doors were open, windows lifted, people stood at the closes and talked. That's how word got round. Neighbourliness can sometimes be taken to mean nosiness but if you know everybody's business you're in a better position to help.

And if things were bad you were never too sad,
At least you were never alone.
No matter the bother, you relied on each other,
For the street took care of its own,
The goodies and baddies, the in-betweens,
The never-will-bes and the never-have-beens,
Gallus courageous, playing their part,
Using the head and sometimes the heart,
In that concrete canyon, asphalt vale,

Already cut off and beyond the pale.
Survivors in that common band,
Safe in their own never-ever land.
The slush, the slime, the sediment,
Nostalgia for a Tenement.

This sort of society is impossible today. Everything has changed. Television has trapped everyone indoors, making them couch captives who know more about people on the screen than they know about the people across the landing. Today, cars clutter the close mouths, which in any case have locked doors across them with security devices into which you have to talk to enter your own close. I know progress has been made but I do feel something very precious has been lost on the way. Something we might never know again.

Now it is rubble
My boyhood home
Nothing of it left
But a vacant space
Devoid of grace
Of all dignity bereft.
A playing field of litter
Rubbish-strewn and bare.
Only the ghost of a building
Now haunts the empty air.

With all the other phantoms
That memory can raise
Shadows from a time gone by
Down the corridor of days
When a warren of homes
Kin-thick and alive
In their man-made mountain
Stone bee-hive
A carousel of families
Going up and down
A street within a village,
A village in a town.

This tapestry of images
Almost lost beyond recall
A living mural drawn in blood
On a gritty greystone wall,
And if it now has returned to dust.
So, in the end, will all of us.
Till then I shall remember
Young days spent
Nostalgia for a Tenement.

Montaigne says, 'The traveller takes himself with him wherever he goes.' I have taken my street image with me around the world. I have rolled up my little strip of asphalt and put it in the memory bag. And when, in some strange land, I take it out and spread it before my mind's eye, the old buildings rise on either side again and people come trooping out the closes. I know these people. I know their houses, each little flat a mirror-image of its tenant, and no two ever the same. I knew them all. Good people and not so good people, but people who are now long dead, or who, like me, have scrawled across the envelope of their minds: 'Gone away. Return to sender.'

Note:
On my last visit to Glasgow, early in 2005, while researching this book, I noticed that my old street bears no name at all on its walls. I asked a man just getting into his car if it was still called Williamson Street. He looked vague. 'I think so,' he said. 'I'm no' sure.'

'Do you live here?' I said.

'Oh ay.' Then he added enigmatically, 'But I'm no' sure.' And drove away at quite a speed.

This is obviously the new kind of tenement dweller: 'Hear no evil, see no evil, do no good.' This small incident reminded of my own brief skirmish with the street name.

In the eighties, when the street was being restored as part of the general reclamation of the East End (GEAR, as mentioned) it was thought that as the character of the street was being so radically altered, a new name was called for. At a meeting of the tenants, or so I was informed, one resident put forward my name as being 'the only wan fae the street that's done somethin' wi' hissel''. This might be open to question, of course, but the motion was carried and the street was to be named for me. I understand it was further carried in the City Chamber Street-Naming Committee on the proposal of Councillor John McQueenie that the street be renamed 'John Cairney Avenue'.

I was asked in an official letter whether I objected to such a proposal. As if I would. Even though I knew, had they lived, that my mother would have been highly embarrassed but my father would have been delighted. My brother only wondered what was wrong with 'James Cairney Avenue'. However, the project foundered on the fracas aroused by the renaming of St George's Place for Nelson Mandela by the then city council and a new rule was brought in denying the naming of any streets for living persons. Now, while I love the idea of my name living on as part of the stonework, I have no desire to hasten such a process by making myself available for martyrdom by masonry, so there the matter must lie.

CHAPTER FOURTEEN

The Flight of the Weegies

AWRABES!

I HAVE SPENT TWO THIRDS of my life away from Glasgow. I have been over the face of the Earth because Stevenson's 'road before me' was that of a travelling actor. Like many other city venturers I flew the nest, or 'shot the craw', as we might have said, as soon as the chance presented it itself early in my career. However, the first, vital part of my life was spent snugly within Glasgow's city boundaries. I say snugly advisedly, because I don't ever remember being hungry as a Glasgow boy, or unloved, or anything less than happy for almost twenty-five years. I'm grateful for that. It could have easily been another story. It's all the luck of the draw – and the parents you are allotted. I had it good.

Apart from annual family holidays to either Ayr or Ireland, I first left Glasgow when I was evacuated during the war. I was given that tantalising, if short, glimpse of the good life lived by some in big country houses that weren't tenements. Later, as a teenager, I was shown the ruins of post-war Germany through the eyes of a National Serviceman in the Royal Air Force, and when I came to London in 1954, that city still belonged to Londoners. I worked there for nearly twenty years before returning to Scotland, but not to Glasgow. Instead, I became a National Trust resident in the East Neuk of Fife and I even had an office in Stevenson's New Town Edinburgh. By this time, I had completely re-invented myself, having been completely 'Anglicised' by the London theatre system of that time, just as that excellent actor, Ian Richardson, (Francis Urquhart) was, although I'm sure I couldn't possibly comment. And even if Ian does come from Edinburgh, he will still retain, like me, what Stevenson called 'a strong Scots accent of the mind'.

I still felt that a wee Glasgow boy was keeking out from behind the theatrical mask. It was more than a Stevensonian duality. I had been so worked over, turned inside out and upside down in the interests of professional survival that I was really a mess of superficial images taking turns in being the front man. Then, for my sixtieth birthday, my wife Alannah gave me the gift of a flying lesson in Glasgow. While soaring over the old Abbotsinch airport, Glasgow re-asserted itself and I decided to be myself. I would preserve that special space within me that was native. That's where I belonged. It would be my own 'carry-on' baggage for the rest of the adventure. I would 'play my ain game' from now on, by the way, but.

I settled in at St Vincent Crescent and started to look around me again from a novel, West End standpoint. I had made many visits to Glasgow during the sixties and seventies, mostly to appear as a spectator at Celtic Park and as a player at the Citizens' Theatre. These stays were enough to give me glimpses of another, emerging Glasgow – almost as if I were seeing it from the windows of a train that was just passing through; but now that I had alighted at Finnieston station, I was resident again.

It was a relief to see that the old Glasgow spark was still there, and I sensed that it could catch fire at any moment. You still had to be careful playing with matches – matches that tried to pair off this volatile flashpoint with equally flash Liverpools, similarly bigoted Belfasts or Birminghams that just went round in circles. It wasn't a Dublin either, although the crack was as good and the singing better. And while the Irish had writers to boast about, most of the great ones were dead. We had filmmakers, and they were very much alive, even if subtitles were required for dead-lazy audiences in Milwaukee. However, even if you only saw it on the big screen, it was obvious that it was the same cheeky

Glasgow face under all the make-up – a face that launched a thousand quips.

My New Zealand emigration in 1991 meant that I had to write this book about Glasgow fourteen years away from her in time and twelve thousand miles in distance. I don't know if either of these conditions lends enchantment, but I do know, as I said, I can still 'feel' Glasgow even if I'm looking out on a flowering jacaranda tree under a near-equatorial sun. I know, even from a distance, that there is still a wee bit of magic hanging over the dear, green place. However, if I can get up close, rather than up a close, I might be able to sum up what it means to me to belong to Glasgow. In other words, to be a Glasgow man – a Weegie.

It's a species which turns up in the most unexpected corners – in a London wine-bar, a Hollywood studio, the sun-deck of a luxury cruise ship, the inner recesses of a doss-house – it's all one to him. The weegie doesn't fly; he hops, from pillar to post and, more than often, from bad to worse. He spreads his wings now and again but it's only for show – he always makes sure that his feet are on the ground. He's lived with the ugly, so he's not put out by it. It's a fact of town life, just as the good bits are – family loyalties, another's love, a child's trust, any welcome surprise in the day. He's learned to take what's on offer – while stocks last. His head constantly bobs on his shoulders as if he is saying, 'Ye know? Ye know?' His hands go palms out to the side as if that explains everything.

He *would* like to fly, but his wings are weighted with centuries of slight. A creature of his size isn't meant to have the aspirations of a hawk or an eagle, so he is left to hop around at ground level as best he can. Over the years he has done this with great effect, mostly in pop music with stars like Lonnie Donegan, an unexpected Glaswegian, but one with all the hallmarks of his kind. Bill Paterson shows it on television and Robert Carlyle does the same in film but Andy Clyde, also from Glasgow, beat him to Hollywood. The type survives in what we know today as the ubiquitous Weegie.

If Edinburgh is famous for its buildings, Glasgow is just as famous for its people. 'We-arra-peep-el' hoarsely exclaimed at the slightest provocation, has little belligerence in it – it is more a triumphant statement of identity. But whose people are they? The answer is their own, for Glasgow's population is as self-made as the city itself. No kings or princes made this place. There is an Earl of Glasgow somewhere, but he wisely keeps a low profile. There are people called Glasgow, but the only one I ever knew was a Geordie.

The Crown Room of Edinburgh Castle displays what are called the Honours of Scotland, the Scottish Regalia of which we are all proud – the Crown, the Sceptre and the Sword of State. Glasgow has no such pearl-imbedded treasures to show from its history but if I were asked to display Glasgow's treasure, I would do as St Lawrence did before the Emperor of Rome many centuries ago. When asked to reveal the treasures of the Church, he went out into the streets and flooded the Emperor's palace with the poor of Rome. He was fried alive for his pains, but if I were asked the same today, I would scour the streets of Glasgow and bring out its people and I would say to the world, 'Here are the Honours of Glasgow, here is its treasure.'

Physically we are all, wherever we come from, the result of all those lives that went into our making ever since Adam, but, just as importantly, we are what we remember. Our individual memories, conscious and subconscious, accrete within us as we grow, and become a force in our development. They will temper our attitude here, adjust it there, and as surely as any sculptor's chisel will permanently form our personality and identity. This is why it matters where a person is born and brought up. Early environment is a potent factor in any life and the circumstances of nurturing can colour your mind just as markedly as your family's genes gave you your nose and the colour of your eyes.

Even weather plays a part in conditioning. Storm winds will bow your head just as a benign sun will lift it. The cold will send you indoors just as warmth will bring you out of yourself. In this way, we become adults via the meteorology of memory. Why do we think it was always sunny when we were young? It must have rained sometime, but childish storms are mostly washed away by the childish tears we must have shed and we are left with the rose-coloured memory of one big juvenile smile.

However, the archaeology of remembering is not at all an exact science. You dig down as far as you can and what comes up differs from spadeful to spadeful. That's what makes it interesting. Our memory of anything is never *exactly* as it was either. Being as it is, a matter of selection, it is a variable phenomenon. There's always a little lie in it. We keep the big lies for things like art – and our age. And whatever age we reach, we have to accept that. Memory is a mischief-maker, an imp of the mind that can play tricks on you. It leaves pictures in the mind to tease you; images that will not go away. They stay with you forever and there's nothing you can do about it. They dart like quicksilver all over your brain but you must go with them. Our memories are our only real possessions, memorials of the mind, where unreason and the dream are legislated to offer a truer representation than any dusty memoir or faded photograph.

The problem is what to do with our bad memories. These also have to be legislated for. Nature supplies its remedy here: amnesia. We tend to forget the bad times – or at least the worst effects of the bad times. It's a survival mechanism, required by everyone, not just Glaswegians. It allows us to sleep at night and braces us for a fresh start in the morning. It's the kind of luggage unwanted on the life voyage, yet it's astonishing how people persist in trailing their sad moments after them, as if they were in a bag that could not be put down. This is the kind of obsession that breeds habits of mind like bias, which, in time, congeals to prejudice. This then stiffens to the granite of bigotry – and we have another statue to an error; one which is hard to topple.

Looking back, however, doesn't get you very far. As a New Zealand writer friend, Karen Curtis, put it, 'You live life forward, but you learn backwards.' The tentacles of the past cling tenaciously, however much we try to shrug them off. It is hard to let go of what has gone before because it has shaped and conditioned who we are today and therefore affects all we might do yet. The pillars of our personal history are nearly always firsts – our first home, our first school, our first sexual experience, our first pay packet, our first home of our own, our first child. These things go deep and they leave their mark, however subconsciously.

They are part of our being and each individual being is part of everybody's. Stand in any crowd and you are sure to find a link somewhere to someone however distant. If we go back far enough we find those who weren't Arabs or Albanians were Jews. Ever since primordial times our bodies have been programmed to survive by genetic replication, so that one can say there is no one in the world that isn't related to someone. We are gene-powered vehicles travelling through time, passing on this bit of information here, letting go of that attribute there, improving our living techniques to keep pace with the world we have made for ourselves. We are trained by nature to live; to breathe in and out, to eat and drink and sleep and propagate. But what is it that makes us want to make poetry, great music, or fine art? It is because, subconsciously or not, we all yearn to go back to the source of all things – whatever you call it. That's the Big Bang that makes us whimper for the impossible. In the meantime, we make the best of what we've got, and going as far back as we can, we try to fathom ourselves in our own beginnings. For me to do so, I have to go back to Glasgow.

Not to go back in time but to go forward, to look towards tomorrow. I want now to move on with the new Glasgow – a Glasgow that goes on. Like the Clyde, it will keep flowing from its source to the wide world beyond. New ideas will come with new times. It is only a matter of time, and energy. And Glasgow's always had bags of that – energy and will. I am sure that Glasgow will go on to become a great European cultural centre by the end of the twenty-first century.

By 2020 it will have the vision and it mustn't lose sight after that. It's all there for it to aim towards; it's only a matter of getting the future in its sights and piling up the necessary ammunition in order to shoot for it. The basics are all there already: the parks and squares, the galleries, the theatres, the concert halls, the arenas; it's only a question of giving the place, as my mother would have called it, a 'good redd-up'. So go to it. Go global. It's all that's left for Glasgow now. I am not a nationalist, or a regionalist. I have a warm feeling for Scotland but I have a deep, ongoing love of Glasgow, especially my little portion in the east. This is only natural, I suppose. It's the place that gave me life. I live because Glasgow, that most alive city, is still alive in me.

And it will be until that old iron bell sounds out its tocsin, the oak tree flowers, the salmon swallows the ring and Weegies fly.

Away!

As a final flourish, I offer you a wee story, a fancy. A Glasgow fairy story, if you like. Just close your eyes and you'll see it better, for this tale, like the bird that never flew or the tree that never grew or the bell that never rang, is about something that never happened. But that doesn't mean it isn't true.

Epilogue: A Glasgow Fancy

A BIG REPRESENTATIVE football match was to be played at the new Hampden Stadium at Mount Florida from twilight time until midnight on the first day of Halloween. Twilight was chosen because it was the magic time; neither day nor night, but a bit of both – the time of two lights when you can never be sure what you're seeing. The teams playing were the Ghosts of Glasgow Past and the Spirits of Glasgow Future. The Ghosts were playing in short shrouds tucked in at the thighs and billowing out on the arms. Their colours were black and blue. Black stripes for the earth from which they'd just come and blue to match their faces. The Spirits were all in white having not made their mark as yet in the world, but they were eager to get on with it in the virtual reality state given to them by the scientists in the main stand.

These same scientists, from the cream of Glasgow's three universities, had whipped up a virtual reality support from some sheep that were still in the labs and were now herded at the King's Park end of the ground already bleating appropriately for the Spirits, waving their virtual reality banners which had nothing written on them because their time had still to come. The Ghosts, however, were old hands at this game. They had been dredged up from burial grounds all over the city. Those from Dalbeth naturally wanted to stand at the other end of the park but the stewards, who had been St Andrew's Ambulance men in the other time, were dead expert at this kind of thing, and got them all in order and everybody in their places. Some of the supporters from the Necropolis looked a bit worse for wear and didn't always have the required supply of arms and legs. Some were even headless but they got the people next to them to tell them what was going on. Anyway, they were able to enjoy all the noise around them. The soundmen in the stand had culled a wonderful ambience from old tapes of big Hampden games in the past and they mixed them to just the right level.

The neutral support – meaning the English-born, the Irish, the Welsh and the Americans, all the Islamic nations in Glasgow who could make it, and a handful of Jamaicans – were all in the Mount Florida stand facing the main stand. They weren't making as much noise as the other ends but they seemed happy enough to be there, even if just out of curiosity. It was noticeable that there were no Chinese in the crowd. They didn't want to take the time off work.

Anyone from the real world looking in on the scene wouldn't have heard a sound or seen a thing, but we know they would have been wrong, don't we? There are times when you have to give in to the unseeable and the unknowable and this Halloween was one of those occasions. It might happen every year for all we know, but you're not likely to get the full report in *The Herald* or the *Daily Record*. This is it as it was. Believe me, I have my sources.

The Glasgow Police Pipe Band emerged on to the field to play as the time neared kick-off. It was hard to know if they were Ghosts or Spirits as they were projected on to the pitch by graphic effect the way they used to do the logos for the TV screens. They sounded fine though a little bit tinny to my ear. 'Scotland the Brave' always goes down well, although 'The Scottish Soldier' didn't do them justice. Still, wee Andy Stewart would have been delighted. Then as the band marched off to the sound of a single drum, the two teams came running out. Well, perhaps not running. Some of them, especially the Ghosts, looked as if they were still carrying injuries, but they were all lifted by the great cheer they received from both sides of the ground. The Spirits were in smart tracksuits, made in China. They were the latest and, being virtual, they of course could have the best. The Ghosts' presentation garb looked more like old burial bags straight from the Royal Crematorium but maybe that was the best they could manage in the time. I noticed they got them off as soon as possible.

The Ghosts were managed by Mr Bill Struth, the famous Rangers manager, because Jock Stein was ineligible being from Burnbank. Mr Struth, who had always been so dapper in his time in his bowler hat and smart suit, must have been appalled at the burial bags; nevertheless he led his team in front of the stand for the presentation. The Spirits were already standing in position. The players were to be introduced to the late, great author, Sir Arthur Conan Doyle, who was from Edinburgh himself but, though he became a doctor, had once played goalkeeper for Portsmouth. He also invented Sherlock Holmes, but these two things were not necessarily connected. Now he came out with all the other officials and dignitaries who looked as specimens of that species do in any age – obsequious yet pompous and always too many of them. However, formalities were completed quickly because the light was already fading and it was time to switch on the fairy lights.

It was then I noticed that the Spirits' manager was a woman, and a young one at that, but she looked very efficient and confident, and I would say, even attractive. No wonder the Spirits looked chirpy. I never caught the young lady's name but then, strictly speaking, she wasn't even born yet. But she shook hands with Mr Struth who doffed his bowler politely to her and escorted her to the tunnel. The teams then stood to attention for the Glasgow anthem, 'I Belong to Glasgow' sung by Will Fyffe himself, who had come that day from Sighthill cemetery, standing on a platform in front of the main stand. Everybody in the ground joined in. It was possibly the only song they all knew except 'My Grannie's Hieland Hame'.

Then came an astonishing item. The Spirits team suddenly lined up across the centre line facing the Ghosts and proceeded to do an energetic line dance with actions based on 'Mhairi's Wedding': 'Step we gaily on we go, heel for heel and toe for toe...' It was the most extraordinary thing I had ever seen in all my years of watching football. It was perhaps an idea borrowed from the New Zealand All Blacks pre-match haka, but there is a big difference between the intimidating Maori challenge and a ponsy 'Mhairi's Wedding'. I think this may have been the young lady's idea. Anyway, the Spirits were as relieved as the rest of us when it was over and the referee, Mr Providence, who was an insurance man in his lifetime, called for the two captains at the centre. Mr Providence was assisted by old Mr Tradition on one touchline and young Mr Posterity on the other.

Captaining the Ghosts was Sir William MacEwan, the famous surgeon who roams the Western (or Westren) in his spare time and had been known to cut through any defence. He played at centre-forward because he admired RS McColl, the prince of centre-forwards and the maker of sweeties. Leading the Spirit clones was a very tall young man who ought to have been a basketball player. He won the toss because he had a close-up of the coin in the air and he chose to play the way he was facing – towards the Aikenhead Road end.

The Ghost team had Nosey Parker in goal (he never let anything get past him); Rabbie (for rabid) Proddie and Stan (for Staunch) Cafflick were at right and left full back (because they kicked with different feet); Midgie Raker was a natural sweeper behind them and Big Rab Haw was at centre-back to gobble up anything around the penalty area. Peter Mannion and Bible John were right and left wing-halves to kill anything that came up the middle and link up with the forwards, especially the wee policeman, Sir Percy Sillitoe, who used all his cunning in dealing with the hard men. Davie Kirkwood, the Beardmore's shop steward before he became a lord, was also very clever at inside and he knew how to get the ball to Sir William MacEwan.

The two wingers were nippy. On the right was Wee Willie Winkie from Tollcross and on the left Pierre Langelier from the Ramshorn Cemetery, where he had been since it was 'Not Proven' in 1857 that Madeleine Smith had put him there. He was a slippery customer and could be a lot of bother on the wing. The trouble with Wee Willie was that he was always checking his clock for the time, but he was nimble. Lobby Dosser was on the bench as twelfth man because he refused to get off his horse, El Fideldo. Rank Badjin was always on his back, which made for a lot of trouble in the dressing room. Mr Struth had his hands full with the Dosser and Wee Winkie.

The Spirits, in contrast, were nameless, belonging as yet to the future. They were so alike you could hardly tell them apart. It was just as well they were numbered. Compared with the motley old Ghosts they were a colourless combination despite the fact they did have a turban or two in their team. This was a strictly functional, robotic unit made entirely to get results and not for idle entertainment. Mr Struth would have seen something of his own wartime Rangers in them.

It was almost seven o'clock of ordinary time when, at last, Mr Providence blew for kick-off. The Spirits went straight into the attack as they always did, anxious to get in quick before proper arrangements to receive them were made. Youth is always in that kind of hurry. But the experience of the Ghosts showed in the way they were able to contain the opening assault. They had seen it all before and just let the youngsters waste a lot of energy in that first ten minutes. Then, against the run of play, the Ghosts scored a goal.

Their first great goal had been the great Exhibitions in Kelvingrove Park in 1901 and they achieved another in 1937 with the Empire Exhibition at Bellahouston. They were now two up on the future and not even half an hour had gone. There was no doubt they had some classy players on their side but they were a mixed bunch and not too well disciplined. It was also a question if their stamina would last. They sagged a bit on the three-quarter mark and lost a penalty because of their carelessness in letting the 'Greek' Thomson buildings deteriorate but the Spirits were too hasty with the resulting kick and the chance to score was lost.

With only ten minutes left in the first half the Ghosts got another goal, a scrambled affair following their expansion in new housing in the post-war boom. The Spirits almost got one back immediately afterwards when most of the high-rise flats in the Gorbals, for which the English architect, Basil Spence, got a knighthood, were blown-up and levelled to the ground, but the referee disallowed it for offside. The Futurists got another score when Charing Cross was ruined and the East End was decimated but the referee chalked this too, for a foul because both incidents were caused by other considerations such as the need for roads. It was a near thing for the Ghosts. Soon afterwards, Providence blew his whistle for the interval and, surprisingly, it was the Spirits who were more relieved to go in for half time re-invigoration by the medical teams.

Interval entertainment was provided by the Glasgow Orpheus Choir, led by their conductor, Sir Hugh Roberton, in select airs which was all very nice and proper. But then the shade of Glen Daly, still in his Ashfield Club gear, then gave a version of what can only be described as Glasgow rap. Tony Capaldi tried to keep up with him on the accordion as Glen gave it laldy on the vocals:

It's a pity that a city gets a name for being shitty
When it's really quite a pleasant looking place,
Yet it's got a name for bein' a locale no' worth the seein'
Which I think, in my opinion's, a disgrace.

Whit's roon aboot the toon will be nae mair fur knockin'
       doon
Bit fur buildin' up and wi' a bit o' pride.
It may no' be the morra, an' it might be a big borra
But I know it's gonna happen on the Clyde.

We kin see it aw a'ready for the progress has been steady
Since first we cleaned the buildin's o' the soot
Wance we cleared aff a' the muck, we could scarce
       believe oor luck
At the difference it made, withoot a doot.

We saw whit we'd been missin' and if anyone'll listen

It's no' the last you'll hear o' Glesca toon,
It knows noo where it's goin' and it only kin go oan
If it ever stoaps fae goin' roon and roon.

If – well, there's a spell when we get it aw tae hell
Then we'll get it right again juist wait an' see
As it says in all the songs, Glesca still belongs
To the people in the street like you an' me.

He then reprised a chorus of 'I Belong to Glasgow' which ended with the crowd in full voice as the teams came out for the second half.

The Spirits started off as they ended the first half with an all-out attack. 'Spirited' was the only word for it, but once again it was the wily Ghosts who scored first. They were awarded a dangerous free kick on the edge of the penalty area for the Pride of Glasgow Event in 1983 and from it got a great direct goal with the Garden Festival. This dampened the Spirits for a bit but they did get one back with the Burrell Collection but their elation over this didn't last long because, within minutes, the Ghosts got the goal of the game so far: the European Year of Culture of 1990. It was a real team effort. Every player seemed to be involved and MacEwan put in the final touch with his usual precision. This made it 5-1 for the Ghosts and it seemed that the Old Guard would easily win the day. But it was not all over yet, by any means.

The Spirits got their act together and they scored again with the House for an Art Lover. This led to an increasing spell of pressure using Mackintosh tactics and, gradually, this ploy paid off with another great goal. This came out of the blue with the refurbishment of Kelvingrove Art Gallery, which nobody had expected. Neither did anyone think they would snatch another goal soon afterwards. It began with a corner they got from gaining the Year of Architecture and Design in 1999 which was based on the building up of the Mackintosh Trail around the city and, from this, their tall captain ran in from the centre line to score with a magnificent header – the restoration of the Art School on Renfrew Street. This rocked the Ghosts who saw that the Spirits now meant business. Their spirit was up and the Ghosts were beginning to feel their lack of body strength. Could their last legs hold out against this Mackintosh-inspired surge? Time was ticking away, and there was now only a goal in it.

There were only five minutes left when the Spirits equalised with a stunner that took one's breath away. This was to apply for World Heritage status for all the Mackintosh sites in and around Glasgow. This goal had such vision, such far-reaching implications for the city, that no defence would have been able to withstand it. Even the neutrals cheered when it was scored and it was evident that, in this epic struggle between the old and the new images, the ancient and modern conceptions, the before and after states, the then and now attitudes, it was anyone's game. Providence had the whistle in his mouth and was looking at his watch. Wee Willie Winkie was protesting that, according to his clock, there was plenty of time left.

It was at this exciting time I had to leave. I had a deadline to meet in the other world and it was something I was contracted to and couldn't get out of. So, very reluctantly, as it got to the eleventh hour, I left them still at it, with extra time looming and the likelihood of penalties deciding it. That would be about right, for both sides were well-matched. Since they are both Glasgow teams, Glasgow itself will win in the end. The Ghosts had achieved a lot in their time and they deserve a little haunting yet, but the Spirits are the coming New Age. They have time on their side and they will not be denied. The great Glasgow has still to be played for and the Futurists know, as we all did in the streets, that the game isn't lost until it's won. It's not Utopia we're talking about here, but Glasgow, by the way but.

Bibliography

Blair, Anna

Tea at Miss Cranston's, London 1985
More Tea at Miss Cranston's, London 1991

Bridie, James

One Way of Living, London 1939

Burrowes, John

Great Glasgow Stories, Edinburgh 1998
Glasgow: Tales of the City, Edinburgh 2001

Brash, Ronald W.

Glasgow in the Tramway Age, London, N/D

Brogan, Colm

The Glasgow Story, London 1952

Cairney, John

East End to West End, Edinburgh 1988
A Wartime Childhood in Glasgow – Stage play for Shanter Productions, 1980 adapted as *Blackout* for Scottish and Canadian Tour, 1983
Nostalgiaglasgow – An after-dinner entertainment, Glasgow 1991
A Scottish Football Hall of Fame, Edinburgh 1998

Chisnall, Edward H.

The Bell in the Tree, Glasgow 1983 & 1984

Cochrane, Hugh

Glasgow: The First 800 Years, Glasgow c. 1975

Crampsey, Bob

The Empire Exhibition 1938, Edinburgh 1988

Daiches, David

Glasgow, London 1977

Fisher, Joe

The Glasgow Encyclopedia, Edinburgh 1904

Foreman, Carol

Did You Know?, Glasgow 1996

Fulton, Rikki

Is it That Time Already?, Edinburgh 1999

Cityfriend Productions Group

Glasgow Guidebook, The, Glasgow 1984

Glasgow Junior Chamber of Commerce,

Glasgow Through A Drinking Glass, Glasgow 1973

Glasser, Ralph	*Gorbals Boy at Oxford*, London 1990
	Growing Up in the Gorbals, London 1986
Gulliver, L.S.	*So This is Glasgow*, Glasgow 1938
Hanley, Cliff	*Dancing in the Streets*, Edinburgh 1983
Hanley, Cliff & Marzaroli, Oscar	*Glasgow: a Celebration*, Edinburgh 1984
House, Jack	*The Heart of Glasgow*, Glasgow 1965
	Music Hall Memories, Glasgow 1986
Irving, Gordon	*The Wit of the Scots*, London 1969
Logan, Jimmy	*It's a Funny Life*, Edinburgh 1998
McGinn, Matt	*Fry the Little Fishes*, London 1975
	McGinn of the Calton, Glasgow 1987
Mackie, Albert D.	*The Scotch Comedians*, Edinburgh 1973
Mitchell, Ian R.	*This City Now*, Edinburgh 2005
Munro, Michael	*The Patter*, Glasgow 1985 & Edinburgh 1988
Murdoch, Helen	*Travelling Hopefully*, Edinburgh 1981
Oakley, C.A.	*The Second City*, London & Glasgow 1946
	Dear Old Glasgow Town, London & Glasgow 1975
Saunders, Donald (ed)	*The Glasgow Diary*, Edinburgh 1984
Struthers, John	*Glasgow's Miles Better*, Glasgow 1986
Ward, Robin	*Some City Glasgow*, Glasgow 1982
Whyte, Hamish (ed)	*Noise and Smoky Breath*, Glasgow 1983
Worsdall, Frank	*A Glasgow Keek Show*, Glasgow 1981

Some other books published by **LUATH** PRESS

The Quest for Charles Rennie Mackintosh
John Cairney
ISBN 1 84282 058 3
HBK £16.99

The Quest for Robert Louis Stevenson
John Cairney
ISBN 0 946487 87 1
HBK £16.99

Art is the flower – Life is the green leaf. Let every artist strive to make his flower a beautiful living thing.
CHARLES RENNIE MACKINTOSH, 1902

For the last thirty years John Cairney has been on a personal quest to find the complex man behind the façade that was Charles Rennie Mackintosh, architect and artist. Though recognised even in his own day as a genius, he was by no means a pre-Raphaelite plaster-cast saint of high morals and mystic vision. He was a flesh and blood charmer, who attracted women as much as he irritated men, enjoyed a drink to a sometimes excessive degree and was known for his explosive temper and black moods. He was all artist, but also all man, with the advantages and disadvantages of both.

This book explores many hitherto unexamined aspects of Toshie's life, delving into the significance of Mackintosh's relationship with his mother, the importance of his first girlfriend, and how much his wife, Margaret Macdonald, contributed to his life.

As the artist Muirhead Bone said of him in 1902: 'To this great artist, someday surely justice will be done.'

In this book John Cairney examines the intimate relationships in the life of Robert Louis Stevenson, and their often destructive effects on his personality and work.

By introducing the boy Stevenson to the terrors of Hell did Alison Cunningham, his Calvinist nanny, irrevocably affect his work as a writer?
What influence did close friends like Charles Baxter, Sidney Colvin, Edmund Gosse, and Fleeming Jenkin have on his development as man and writer?
What was it that drove Stevenson to burn the first draft of *The Strange Case of Dr Jekyll and Mr Hyde*?
Why did RLS lose his closest friend and could it have been prevented?
Might there have been more to his relationship with his faithful stepdaughter and secretary Belle?

A compelling read, *The Quest for Robert Louis Stevenson* sheds new light on the complicated life of the man behind the famous stories – *Treasure Island*, *The Strange Case of Dr Jekyll and Mr Hyde* and *Kidnapped*.

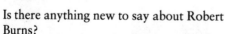

On the Trail of Robert Burns
John Cairney
ISBN 0 946487 51 0
PBK £7.99

Immortal Memories
John Cairney
ISBN 1 84282 009 5
HBK £20.00

Is there anything new to say about Robert Burns?

John Cairney says it's time to trash Burns the Brand and come on the trail of the real Robert Burns. He is the best of traveling companions on this convivial, entertaining journey to the heart of the Burns story.

Internationally known as 'the face of Robert Burns', John Cairney believes that the traditional Burns tourist trail urgently needs to find a new direction. In an acting career spanning forty years he has often lived and breathed Robert Burns on stage. *On the Trail of Robert Burns* shows just how well he has got under the skin of Burn's complex character. This fascinating journey around Scotland is a rediscovery of Scotland's national bard as a flesh and blood genius.

On the Trail of Robert Burns outlines five tours, mainly in Scotland. Key sites include:

Alloway – Burn's birthplace. Tam O' Shanter draws on the Alloway Kirk witch-stories first heard by Burns in his childhood.

Mossgiel – Between 1784 and 1786 in a phenomenal burst of creativity Burns wrote some of his most memorable poems including Holy Willie's Prayer and To a Mouse.

Kilmarnock – The famous Kilmarnock edition of Poems Chiefly in the Scottish Dialect published in 1786.

Edinburgh – Fame and Clarinda (among others) embraced him.

Dumfries – Burns died at age 37. The trail ends at the Burns mausoleum in St Michael's churchyard.

A Compilation of Toasts To the Immortal Memory of Robert Burns as delivered at Burns Suppers around the world together with other orations, verses and addresses 1801 – 2001.

The annual Burns Supper, held on or around his birthday, January 25, has become something of a cult in virtually every country in the world where 'Scottish' is spoken – and even where it is not. This is an occasion when people gather around a dinner table to give tribute to a Scottish poet who died more than two hundred years ago. It really is an extraordinary phenomenon.

Thus begins John Cairney's latest work focusing on Scotland's national bard, Robert Burns. To be asked to deliver the 'Immortal Memory', the chief toast and centrepiece of the traditional Burns Supper, is recognised as a privilege cherished by Burns enthusiasts the world over. Immortal Memories is an extensive collection of these toasts, spanning two hundred years from the first Burns Supper in Alloway in 1801 to the Millennium Burns Suppers of 2001.

The Luath Burns Companion
John Cairney
ISBN 1 84282 000 1
PBK £10.00

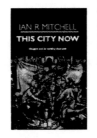

This City Now
Ian R. Mitchell
ISBN 1 84282 082 6
PBK £12.99

'Robert Burns was born in a thunderstorm and lived his brief life by flashes of lightning.' So says John Cairney in his introduction. In those flashes his genius revealed itself.

This collection is not another 'complete works' but a personal selection from 'The Man Who Played Robert Burns'. This is very much John's book. His favourites are reproduced here and he talks about them with an obvious love of the man and his work. His depth of knowledge and understanding has been garnered over forty years of study, writing and performance.

The collection includes sixty poems, songs and other works; and an essay that explores Burns' life and influences, his triumphs and tragedies. This informed introduction provides the reader with an insight into Burns's world.

Burns's work has drama, passion, pathos and humour. His careful workmanship is concealed by the spontaneity of his verse. He was always a forward thinking man and remains a writer for the future.

This City Now sets out to retrieve the hidden architectural, cultural and historical riches of some of Glasgow's working-class districts. Many who enjoy the fruits of Glasgow's recent gentrification will be surprised and delighted by the gems which Ian Mitchell has uncovered beyond the usual haunts.

An enthusiastic walker and historian, Mitchell invites us to recapture the social and political history of the working-class in Glasgow, by taking us on a journey from Partick to Rutherglen, and Clydebank to Pollokshaws, revealing the buildings which go unnoticed every day yet are worthy of so much more attention.

Once read and inspired, you will never be able to walk through Glasgow in the same way again.

Mitchell is a knowledgable, witty and affable guide through the streets of the city.
GREEN LEFT WEEKLY

The Glasgow 100
David Phillips
ISBN 1 84282 068 0
PBK £4.99

Monsieur Mackintosh
Robin Crichton
ISBN 1 905222 36 X
PBK £15.00

A new [4th] edition of the popular Glasgow restaurant guide, previously known as the *Evening Times* 'Eating Out in Glasgow' review. A lively and impartial guide to 100 places to eat out. Anonymous appraisals (David Phillips is not his real name!) ensure independence.

Covering the West End, the City Centre, Merchant City and East Glasgow, and the South Side.

In 1923, Charles Rennie Mackintosh and his wife Margaret Macdonald went on holiday to Roussillon, in the South of France, to rest and recuperate. Her health was poor and as an architect and designer he had become outmoded. They were enchanted. The holiday became a permanent stay and Mackintosh rapidly developed his talents as an artist. They spent the last and possibly the happiest years of their life together in this earthly paradise, which is Roussillon.

Robin Crichton, President of the Association CRM en Roussillon, follows in Mackintosh's footsteps, rediscovering as he did the culture and beauty of the region and how it inspired his painting. Crichton's own love of Roussillon shines through, and his elegiac prose sits in perfect harmony with Mackintosh's splendid paintings.

...beautifully illustrated book...Crichton's bilingual French-English text draws on Mackintosh's own letters and journals to offer some touching insights into the restorative capacities capacities of both travel and art.
THE SCOTSMAN

Singin I'm No A Billy He's A Tim
Des Dillon
ISBN 1 905222 27 0
PBK £6.99

The Glasgow Dragon
Des Dillon
ISBN 1 84282 056 7
PBK £9.99

What happens when you lock up a Celtic fan? What happens when you lock up a Celtic fan with a Rangers fan? What happens when you lock up a Celtic fan with a Rangers fan on the day of the Old Firm match? Des Dillon creates the situation and watches the sparks fly as Billy and Tim clash in a rage of sectarianism and deep-seated hatred. When children have been steeped in bigotry since birth, is it possible for them to change their views?

Contains strong language.

A humorous and insightful look at the bigotry that exists between Glasgow's famous football giants Celtic and Rangers.
RICHARD PURDEN

Nothing is as simple as good and evil.

When Christie Devlin goes into business with a triad to take control of the Glasgow drug market little does he know that his downfall and the destruction of his family is being plotted. As Devlin struggles with his own demons the real fight is just beginning.

There are some things you should never forgive yourself for.
Will he unlock the memories of the past in time to understand what is happening?
Will he be able to save his daughter from the danger he has put her in?

Des Dillon's turn at gangland thriller is an intelligent, brutal and very Scottish examination of the drug trade.
THE LIST

Me and Ma Gal
Des Dillon
ISBN 1 84282 054 0
PBK £5.99

A sensitive story of boyhood friendship told with irrepressible verve.

Me an Gal showed each other what to do all the time, we were good pals that way an all. We shared everthin. You'd think we would never be parted. If you never had to get married an that I really think that me an Gal'd be pals for ever. That's not to say that we never fought. Man we had some great fights so we did. The two of us could fight just about the same but I was a wee bit better than him on account of ma knowin how to kill people without a gun an all that stuff that I never showed him.

Des Dillon perfectly captures the essence of childhood. He explores the themes of lost innocence, fear and death, writing with subtlety and empathy.

Reminded me of Twain and Kerouac... a story told with wonderful verve, immediacy and warmth.
EDWIN MORGAN

Broomie Law
Cinders McLeod
ISBN 0 946487 99 5
PBK £4.00

A dry look at life in today's Britain through the eyes of a five year old street prophet.

Named after the heart of Glasgow's docks, Broomie Law and her Glasgow-namesake-sidekicks – Annie Land, Molly Cate, Mary Hill and Hag's Castle – have searched for truth, justice and not the third way, for four years in the *Glasgow Herald*.

Broomie Law is fab.
ALEX SALMOND, MP

Cinders is a great cartoonist and helps us to see the truth behind the facade.
TONY BENN

She's that rare creature: a woman and a cartoonist of perceptive wit. Now Cinders McLeod enters a city's heart.
RON CLARK, THE HERALD

Broomie's handbag packs as great a punch as Lobey Dosser's revolver once did in the Evening Times.
ELSPETH KING, STIRLING SMITH ART GALLERY AND MUSEUM

Driftnet
Lin Anderson
ISBN 1 84282 034 6
PBK £9.99

Talking with Tongues
Brian D. Finch
ISBN 1 84282 006 0
PBK £8.99

A driftnet catches everything.

A young rent boy is found strangled and mutilated in a Glasgow flat. Leaving her warm bed and lover in the middle of the night to take forensic samples from the body, Rhona MacLeod immediately recognises the likeness between herself and the dead boy and is horrified to think that he might be the son she gave up for adoption sixteen years before.

Amidst the turmoil of her own love life and consumed by guilt from her past, Rhona sets out to find the boy's killer and her own son. But the powerful men who use the Internet paedophile ring to trawl for vulnerable boys have nothing to lose and everything to gain from Rhona MacLeod's death.

Poetry from Glasgow bus driver Brian D. Finch.

I have read [Talking with Tongues] with much interest. The language component is strong, but so is the sense of history, and indeed the whole book is a vigorous reminder of how linguistically orientated Scottish poetry has been over the centuries. It revives, in fact, the medieval macaronic tradition in a modern and witty fashion. The range of reference from Anerin to Desert Storm is good for opening the mind and scouriing it out a bit.
EDWIN MORGAN

Brian D Finch is a 'talker' of note in a city of eloquent tongues, whether in the convival surroundings of Tennent's Bar or as the accomplished poet of this collection... He feels passionately about the obscenities of modern life, composing an almost public poetry in the time-honoured Scottish tradition, yet retaining throughout an outstanding sense of humour and an ever-present awareness of the ridiculous.
TED COWAN